SOPHIE GRIGSON'S
SUNSHINE FOOD

SOPHIE GRIGSON'S
SUNSHINE FOOD

Food photography by Georgia Glynn-Smith

This book is published to accompany the television series *Sophie Grigson's Sunshine Food*, which was produced by BBC Birmingham.

Series Producer: Mary Clyne
Director: Nicola Silk

Published by BBC Worldwide Ltd, Woodlands, 80 Wood Lane, London W12 0TT

First published 2000
© Sophie Grigson 2000
The moral right of the author has been asserted.

Food photography © Georgia Glynn-Smith 2000

ISBN 0 563 55169 0

Commissioning Editor: Nicky Copeland
Project Editor: Sarah Miles
Copy Editor: Deborah Savage
Art Director: John Calvert
Picture Researchers: David Cottingham and
    Charlotte Lochhead
Home Economist: Maxine Clark
Stylist: Róisín Nield

Set in Helvetica Neue
Printed and bound in Great Britain by Butler & Tanner Ltd, Frome, Somerset
Colour separations by Radstock Reproductions Ltd, Midsomer Norton
Jacket printed by Lawrence Allen Ltd, Weston-super-Mare

To Mary C, Queen of the Courgettes, Señora de los Boquerones, Suora Maria

CONTENTS

INTRODUCTION

If I were asked to describe my ideal holiday place, my answer would run something like this: first of all, it must be warm and sunny; and I would like a sandy beach, with not too many people on it, but with a small bar and an unpretentious little restaurant; then, absolutely crucially, there must be ruins and local markets and narrow old streets to wander through, nearby. The hotel or house doesn't have to be grand, and it certainly won't be one of those big, concrete-block holiday complexes that ruin the view from the beach. Something simple, clean and with a good view from the window will do me nicely. And one last item on my list – the food must be good, again not grand, but made with fresh local ingredients, cooked without fuss and frills, but with care and love. Now that's not a lot to ask for, is it?

Around the lengthy shores of the Mediterranean sea, 'the sea in the centre of the earth', there are still places that fulfil most of my criteria for a perfect holiday. Sadly, it is now hard (but not impossible) to find an almost empty beach and big, concrete-block hotels have mushroomed like some fungal disease, but sun, sea, interesting sights and good food are a quartet that seem to go hand in hand.

The lands of the Mediterranean, from Spain sweeping round in a grand circle through the South of France, Italy, Greece, and Turkey, the Lebanon, Israel, and on into North Africa – Egypt, Tunisia and on finally to Morocco – are immensely seductive to us Northerners. The magic begins as we step off the plane or train, to be bathed in warmth and that extraordinary, glittering, crystal light. When I back-packed around Europe in my late teens and early twenties, often taking the overnight train from Paris down to Rome, I always savoured those first few minutes on Mediterranean soil, before heading straight into the station buffet, for a short, dark, electrifying espresso coffee at the bar, and a bite to eat. Continental station buffets have much more to offer than their British equivalents. It was in stations that I took my first bites of Sicilian *arancini* (balls of rice filled with peas and cheese), Italian frittata sandwiches (for more on these turn to page 76), Spanish *churros* (breakfast doughnuts, sprinkled with sugar), and Greek *souvlakia* (see page 144), amongst others. With my craving for that taste of the Mediterranean satisfied, I could then lean back against the bar (cheaper than sitting at a table – very important when you are a student) and savour the everyday sights and sounds of the Mediterranean:

families passing through with gaggles of children, workers stopping in for a quick chat and a quick pick-me-up, before shouting their goodbyes and traipsing off back to work, older men playing cards in a corner, a pair of besuited business men arguing a deal, and the sun streaming in.

The food of the Mediterranean countries has fascinated me since long before I started to write about food as a career. When I was fourteen, my parents took me to Greece on a working holiday – my father was writing a book about the goddess Aphrodite. I may have been at that age when anything parents do is embarrassing but even mid-teenage sulks didn't spoil the thrill of it all. And the things I remember above all are the flavours of the foods, many totally new to me. In those days, Greek yoghurt was almost unknown in Britain, so the bowls of thick, creamy yoghurt, with a crinkling cream crust, drizzled with honey, were a revelation. I tasted real taramasalata on the top of Lykabetus in Athens, a country salad with feta cheese and crisp cos lettuce by the ruins of Epidauros, char-grilled fish with lemon, olive oil and *rígani* (dried wild oregano) at Paphos in Cyprus, hard by the beach where Aphrodite is said to have emerged from the sea on her scallop shell.

In the intervening years, I have continued my love affair with the blessed countries that cluster around their Mediterranean sea, travelling around whenever I can. The area is linked not only by a stretch of water but also by certain basic ingredients. You could almost define the Mediterranean lands by the cultivation of olive trees and the use of olive oil (as long as you ignore – as I shall for the time being – the fact that both South Africa and Australia are now producing superb olive oil). The visitor is never far from these graceful trees, with their grey green leaves. To go with the golden green oil of life, there are nearly always lemons, their acid yellow warmed by the sunlight, their sharp juice waiting to bring life and freshness to any number of dishes. Tomatoes, late arrivals that they were, have conquered the terrain entirely, whilst aubergines, courgettes and sweet peppers are universally loved. The lengthy shoreline ensures that fish are on the menu as often as, if not more frequently than, meat. The warm sun caresses fruit trees into producing fruit so juicy, sweet and ecstatically fragrant that puddings take second place.

What never ceases to amaze me is the inventiveness of Mediterranean cooks. Each time I visit, even if only for a few short days, I discover new ways of manipulating common foodstuffs, to transform them into something distinctive and delicious. Of course, they are lucky in that they still have easy access to first-class ingredients, though kitchens may often lack all the sophisticated gadgetry that we take for granted. Take a trip to a market, anywhere around the area, and the inspiration for culinary endeavour is all around you. What joy to be able to take, say, the fruit and vegetable market of Nice, or the fish market in Cadiz, or the provisions market of Tel Aviv, for granted – I'd swap that any day for the gizmos of a British kitchen.

Just as fascinating are the similarities of certain dishes in different countries. These are amongst the most visible remnants of conquering armies, ancient trading routes and great civilizations. Dishes like couscous, a North African speciality, with variations right through Morocco, Algeria and Tunisia, resurface in Sicily and elsewhere, modified by time and local ingredients but still recognizable.

I always return heavily laden from voyages abroad, as my travelling companions will confirm. Photos are lovely, and bring back happy days and spectacular places, but I like something more tangible and, in particular, pots and bowls and jugs. But if circumstance dictates that I must travel light (loathsome notion), then I also bring back something else that can be made tangible, something far more evocative than photos or crocks. Recipes.

With a recipe, you can, in theory, recreate the smells and flavours of another land and, as everyone knows, smell – above all other senses – is the most powerful trigger to recalling memories of the past. Recreating a meal you've enjoyed while abroad, sharing it with friends or family, somehow lengthens the pleasures of travel, bringing them right into your own daily reality. But it is not always as easy as it might appear. Even if you have been able to persuade your hosts to part with precise details of how this or that dish was made, the results can be less than impressive. The reasons are not difficult to fathom. For all our sophisticated supermarkets, packed to the hilt with ingredients from the world over, what we lack is that simple Mediterranean market, which has barely changed over centuries. We are deprived of access to the tomatoes grown under the sun at full throttle and picked that morning, the hand-cured local hams, the bread

baked by a skilled baker in an antiquated wood-fired oven, the farmer's home-made cheese from the flock of goats he tends himself. Instead, we have to make the most of what we do have, and encourage our producers to increase their expertise, to bring us better produce, to encourage individuality not uniformity. Supermarkets are now superbly well stocked with imported ingredients from the Mediterranean, but it would be good to see them working side by side with the small guys, so that we customers can have the best of both worlds.

In the meantime, the aim of this book is to bring back to Britain some of that marvellous cooking that I've loved so much over the course of my travels. I've adapted recipes where necessary, to square with the kind of ingredients we can get relatively easily, and I suggest alternatives to some ingredients, where the original is unobtainable here. Most of the recipes are pretty quick and easy, but there's an occasional side-step to something more complicated (though never very technically demanding) or lengthy, to keep you on your toes. I would love to attempt a more comprehensive guide to the cooking of the Mediterranean, but I doubt that I would ever be able to finish it, let alone persuade a publisher to publish the tomes that would be necessary to do the subject justice. So, failing that, this offering is merely a selection of some of my favourite dishes, some well known, others less so but just as good. It has been an incredible pleasure to compile and I hope that you will find things in it that will give you some measure of that pleasure.

Ciao,

Sophie

BUYING SUNSHINE IN A COOL CLIMATE:
A DIRECTORY OF MEDITERRANEAN INGREDIENTS

This is by no means an exhaustive list of the best of Mediterranean ingredients – it would take several volumes even to approach that – but this directory does cover many of the most important Mediterranean ingredients that appear in the recipes in this book, along with information on buying and preparing them where relevant.

Air-dried Hams: Air-dried hams, or in other words raw, cured hams are big business in Italy and Spain, as well as, to a lesser extent, in France. These are hams that are cured by rubbing with salt, often mixed with a whole host of other ingredients – spices, herbs, sugar, molasses, vinegar and so on – then

hung up to dry over a period of months, if not years. The effect of the cure and the drying is to render them entirely safe (bacteria cannot thrive in this inhospitable climate) and extremely good to eat, when they are treated rightly.

In Italy, this type of ham is known as *prosciutto crudo*, or often just prosciutto (cooked ham is *prosciutto cotto*) and the most famous of them all is Parma ham (*prosciutto di Parma*). Parma ham is salted for between 15 and 25 days and then hung up to dry for some 14 months. San Daniele ham has a slightly shorter drying time but is considered by connoisseurs of Italian hams to be just as good as Parma ham. Both are protected by law, and can only be made with the best quality hams, from a specific area and in a specific, traditional

way. Second-rate hams are rejected and cannot be sold under either name.

There is one other, increasingly highly rated, air-dried ham, and that is the Spanish *jamón serrano*, mountain ham. The best is made up in the hills of the Sierra de Aracena in south-west Spain, from the meat of the black-footed Iberian pig. Like Parma ham, at its best it has a marvellous sweetness that balances the salt of the cure.

Most of the air-dried ham that we buy here comes pre-sliced in vacuum packs, which does it no favours but is better than nothing, and certainly fine for cooking with. If you ever get a chance to try them cut fresh from the ham (at right angles to the bone for Italian hams, parallel to it for Spanish), you will instantly notice a difference.

Almonds: If you want almonds to taste really, really almondy – assuming you don't have an almond grove in your back garden – buy them unblanched, in their brown skins. You don't find them like this in supermarkets much any more, so you will have to head off to a whole food or health food shop. To skin them, cover with boiling water, leave them for a minute and then drain and squeeze the almonds out of their skins. What? You haven't got time? You can't be doing with all that? Oh, okay then, I admit that I don't do it that often either... but for a special occasion it is definitely worth your while.

Anchovies: These small, silvery fish, rarely more than 10 cm (4 inches) long, make very good eating when fresh, though they're an uncommon treat in Britain. Since they begin to deteriorate very quickly after they have been caught, the vast majority of the haul is preserved under salt, just as it has been for centuries. The entire body of the anchovy is salted (sometimes headed and gutted, sometimes whole) and, if you wander through Mediterranean markets, you will often see them displayed in open tins or wooden barrels, the salt crystals clinging to their silvery and rust curves. You may come across smaller tins of salted anchovies in Greek and Turkish stores in this country. These more mature, salted anchovies have a fantastic flavour but need to be rinsed thoroughly, filleted and soaked in milk or water to draw some of the salt.

For most of us who cook here, anchovies means tinned anchovies in oil, which rate high upon the list of essential, high-quality store-cupboard items in my kitchen. Look for anchovies in olive oil – the quality and type of oil obviously affects the flavour. As well as being a welcome addition in some salads, on savoury tarts and *Pissaladière* (see page 94), they can also be used as a background flavour. Fry roughly chopped anchovies in a little olive oil (and throw in a chopped garlic clove, too, for good effect), and you'll see that they begin to dissolve into the oil, helped along a little by mashing down with a fork, to form a rough purée. This mixture of garlic and anchovy oil makes a good dressing for pasta all on its own but can also make the basis of a brilliant tomato sauce to serve with meat or fish.

Marinated, silvery anchovies, often sold now in delicatessens, taste very different: sharper, but at the same time softer and much, much less salty. They can be served just as they are, perhaps with a salad of tomatoes or cucumber, with good bread, as an hors d'oeuvre, or arranged over salads of grilled peppers, or lettuce and cooked vegetables.

Arborio Rice: see Rice.

Balsamic Vinegar: see Vinegar.

Basil: Italy's most renowned herb, sweet, fragrant, peppery, thrilling basil, actually originated in India. But the

Italians have adopted it lock, stock, and barrel, trumpeting its starry marriage with the tomato and creating a sauce that shows it off at its most brilliant: pesto, which has now become an international megastar. I love basil but, sadly, there is basil and then there is basil and the two are not necessarily the same. Basil grown outdoors, under a mercilessly strong sun, has a peppery intensity that can set the pulse racing. Basil that has been grown under glass, in cooler climates, will look just as good, if not better, but can only compete in the tamest of ways. Most of what we can buy at home, or indeed can grow at home, will taste and smell pretty good, but doesn't reach superstar status. There's little you can do to change that, short of getting your basil flown over from Italy in the summer, and doing without in the winter.

Grow your own basil if you can, otherwise buy it in bunches or plastic packs. Avoid the 'growing basil' sold in pots in supermarkets – it rarely has any flavour at all.

Basmati Rice: see Rice.

Bulgar: Bulgar, or burgul or any one of a number of spellings of a similar kind, is actually dried, cracked wheat. It has already been cooked before dehydrating, so all it needs is rehydrating before it's ready to use. I mix roughly equal quantities of hot water and bulgar and then leave it to soak and soften for 15 minutes or so before draining off any excess water. This can then form the basis for a salad, with oodles of chopped herbs, finely diced tomato, cucumber, spring onions or whatever, or can be heated up, with plenty of butter, to serve as a side-dish. Bulgar wheat is now sold by many supermarkets and the vast majority of health food shops.

Capers: Capers are the pickled buds of a plant that grows amongst rocks all around the shores of the Mediterranean. The smaller they are, the better, with the teensiest dots of capers known as 'nonpareils'. The majority of the capers sold here are bottled in vinegar or brine, giving them a tart flavour which I like, particularly with fish, but you can also buy them salted which some aficionados insist are far superior. I'm not entirely convinced; I just think they are different, equally as good, and aren't we lucky to have two products to choose from rather than one? If you do use salted capers, you will need to rinse them thoroughly and then possibly also soak them for 20

minutes in cold water to draw out more of the salt. Let your mouth be your guide in this – tasting is the only way to find out if they are ready to use.

Cavolo Nero: *Cavolo nero* just about pips savoy cabbage to the Miss Cabbage World Beauty contest first prize. Its tall, black-green leaves rise up and curl like Prince of Wales feathers, the most elegant cabbage you are ever likely to come across. It is widely grown and used in Tuscany, where it features in

soups such as their *Zuppa di Verdura* and *Ribollita* (see pages 26 and 27), as well as being served as a vegetable in its own right. Its taste is almost meaty and not too vehemently cabbagey, while the leaves have a firm texture. It can be simmered in salted water and then be served plain, with just a drizzle of olive oil, but I think it is at its best as a side-dish when braised. Cover the base of a wide deep frying-pan with a good coating of olive oil and then pack the shredded *cavolo nero* leaves in and scatter over a few cloves of garlic, sliced. Add a splash or two of water, salt and pepper, cover tightly and leave to cook over a low heat for about 10 minutes, more if it needs it. Check the cabbage every now and then, turning it so that it cooks evenly and adding a splash more water if it is threatening to catch. When it is tender, squeeze over some lemon juice, cover again and leave for a final minute or two before serving.

Cavolo nero is slowly becoming available in this country, from more upmarket supermarkets and greengrocers but, if you really can't get it, the runner up, savoy cabbage, or curly kale (which

comes in third place in the beauty contest, I reckon) can be used instead in Italian recipes, adjusting cooking times accordingly.

Chickpeas: Chickpeas are of considerable culinary importance in Spain and North Africa, where they appear in soups, stews (*cocidos* and couscous), fritters such as *Falafel* (see page 39) and purées such as hummus. The most economical way to buy them is dried. Dried chickpeas have a better flavour than tinned ones, but they demand more attention. First they must be soaked for at least 8 hours or overnight, otherwise they will never, ever soften, and then they need boiling hard for 10 minutes, followed by one or more hours in the pot. Really dry, old chickpeas can take as long as 2½ hours to simmer to a proper tenderness. As with all pulses, don't add salt or anything acidic, such as lemon juice or tomato, to the pan, or they will stay resolutely tough and chewy. Lucky cooks in Spain and Morocco don't have to go through all of this palaver; they can just buy them ready-cooked (but not tinned) in markets.

Chickpea flour is used in Italy and the South of France to make very moreish savoury 'pancakes' (see page 32). It can be bought in Italian delicatessens, where it will be labelled *farina di ceci* or from Indian food stores, where it is sold as 'gram flour'.

Chorizo: The Spanish answer to salami, chorizo is a cured pork sausage, flavoured with paprika – which gives it an orange colour – as well as other herbs and spices. Chorizo can either be mild (*dulce*) or hot (*piccante*). The larger, air-dried sausages are sliced thinly and eaten with drinks or as a first course, with other cured meats and cheeses, or in sandwiches made with sturdy bread. There is also a softer form of chorizo, shaped like a plump British sausage, that has only been semi-cured, making it ideal for cooking. These are sometimes just grilled or fried and served as they are, again with good bread to mop up the orange juices, or used to flavour stews, or fried dishes. Chorizo may well go into a paella or other rice dish, or be fried up with vegetables.

Coriander Leaves: The Mediterranean countries can be split pretty neatly into those that don't and those that do. The don'ts lie, for the most part, to the north. A sighting of a leaf of coriander on the dinner plate is a rare thing indeed in Italy,

France or Spain. Portugal is the exception, but then it is hardly a Mediterranean country, with its lengthy Atlantic coast. You have to travel south to northern Africa to find the truly remarkable, entrancing flavour of coriander, which grows upon you stealthily until you become quite addicted to it.

These days there is absolutely no problem buying coriander in our local shops, I'm glad to say. In fact, in supermarkets it is now the second-biggest-selling herb after parsley. Amazing when you think that only twenty or so years ago it was virtually unknown here. Try, if you can, to buy coriander from smaller Greek, Turkish, Asian or West Indian food stores, where coriander is, quite rightly, sold in beautiful big bunches for a song. Some supermarkets are now following their lead but, even so, their bunches are on the puny side in comparison. Don't stand the coriander in a glass of water on the window sill when you get home, not if you want it to last any time, that is. Pop it instead in an airtight container in the vegetable drawer of the fridge and pick it over daily, discarding any yellowing leaves.

Although there are plenty of instances where coriander is simmered into stews and sauces, I've always found this to be a total waste of time. You lose that strange and wonderful flavour that makes coriander so beguiling, and I can never detect anything much in taste terms to make up for the loss. Better to strew it on to dishes liberally at the end of the cooking time, or to process big handfuls into sauces or soups, or to toss it gleefully into salads.

Coriander Seeds: With the seed of the coriander plant, we find full Mediterranean consensus. Everybody loves it, everybody uses it without hesitation. It has a distinctly orangey aroma that marks it out from other spices. Though the aroma is clear it is never domineering, blending subtly with other ingredients, particularly vegetables (a ratatouille isn't a proper ratatouille unless it is sown generously with coriander seeds) and meat. It is thrown into marinades and pickles and breath-freshening mixes. Like nearly all spices, coriander seed is best bought whole and then ground to a powder if necessary, when it is needed. To extract the maximum aroma, dry-fry the seeds briefly and then cool and crush coarsely in a mortar, or grind to a powder.

Couscous: Morocco, Tunisia and Algeria's favourite staple, couscous is not actually a grain, but a minuscule form of pasta. In the old days, it used to be made laboriously by hand, tiny nubbles of semolina rolled in semolina flour to form the pin-head pellets. The traditional way to cook it is to steam it over a simmering stew (which will be served with the couscous, at which point the combined dish of both stew and staple is called couscous, just to confuse you), repeatedly lifting it off and rubbing it with 'smen' (aged butter), to break up any lumps, and then continuing with the steaming. Modern cooks, however, are saved from this laborious task. These days most of the couscous you can buy has already been cooked and simply needs rehydrating with hot water (equal volumes of water and couscous). Add salt, and work some butter through it, and it is ready to eat, though I think it better for a touch of steaming – in other words, I tip it into a shallow dish, season and dot it generously with butter, or drizzle olive oil over it and then cover with foil and leave in a low oven for about 20 minutes. Then all it needs is forking through to fluff it up, before serving. It isn't, I have to admit, quite as good as the slowly cooked and lovingly tended traditional couscous, but the small loss in flavour and texture is more than made up for by the speed with which it can be prepared.

Crème Fraîche: While the French are busy envying us our single, whipping and double cream, we lust after their crème fraîche. So much so that we bring over vats of it to feed our lust, and have even started to make it here. Far more than mere soured cream, it is very rich and thick, with a lemony tang that makes it a wonderful accompaniment to sweet puddings. It is also perfect for cooking and making quick sauces (deglaze a pan after frying meat or fish with a slug of white wine or other booze and, when it has boiled down a bit, add plenty of crème fraîche and boil down to a good, sauce-like consistency) because it doesn't curdle, thanks to its ridiculously high butter fat content. Crème fraîche is not for calorie-counters or cholesterol-watchers but for a treat every once in a while it's hard to beat.

Cumin: One of the most evocative and inspiring of all spices, the aroma of cumin instantly conjures up pictures of exotic locations, the markets of North Africa, the Middle East and India. You can more or less track the movements of the Moors around the Mediterranean, and further afield, by the taste of cumin. It frequently appears in the cooking of Southern Spain, pops up again in parts of Italy, and then from Greece round to Morocco it is used with increasing regularity. Although most Moroccan recipes for tagines and couscous dishes call for ground cumin, like all spices it makes much more sense to buy whole cumin seeds, so that its full flavour is captured, ready to be released only when you grind it to a powder just before using it. Dry-frying it first makes it easier to grind and enhances the flavour. Ready-ground cumin loses much of its zip within a matter of weeks. Cumin is a magic spice used solo, but also a capital team member, cropping up in endless spice mixes.

Cumin Salt: This is put on to the table to season food. It is just equal quantities of ground cumin and salt, mixed together. It is sometimes put into one of those mini-tagines, whilst another may contain cayenne pepper.

Dried Mushrooms: see Porcini.

Feta Cheese: This is the one Greek cheese that everyone, or at least everyone with an interest in food, knows, though there are many others produced all around the country. It is a brined sheep's milk cheese, preserved in a soup of salty liquid so that it never loses that milky taste. Inevitably it is rather salty, so needs to be used almost as a condiment, to season and add its sharp-salt tang to dishes of vegetables, savoury pastries and pies.

Filo Pastry: So thin you can read a newspaper through it – that's what the expert makers of tissue-paper-fine filo pastry aim for. Filo and its cousins, *warka* and *malsouka* pastry, are used right around the eastern and southern Mediterranean from Greece to Morocco to create heavenly, crisp, flaky pastries, both savoury and sweet. Filo is the only one of these that is readily available (from most supermarkets and all Greek/Turkish food shops, either fresh or frozen) in this country. It is easy to use, as long as you follow a few basic rules. The first and most crucial is that you must keep the filo from drying out as you work with it. The moment it dries it becomes brittle and crumbles at a finger's touch. So, take only what you need from the box, seal what is left in cling film, and return immediately to the fridge, or freeze. I usually cover the pile of sheets of filo I'm working with, with a sheet of greaseproof paper, and lay a tea-towel wrung out in cold water over that but, if I'm in a hurry and there's not an awful lot of filo to protect, I may just cover it with a sheet of cling film.

To turn it crisp, yet keep it sturdy in the oven, brush each sheet lightly with melted butter or olive oil. Once the pastry is formed, you no longer need to worry about it drying out.

If you are using a dampish filling (such as the egg filling on page 74), work quickly and get your pastries into the oven or fat before the pastry softens and tears. Most of the time, fillings will be more solid, more of a thick purée, or even dry, in which case there is nothing to worry about. In fact, if the filling can take it, you can hold the pastries in the fridge for several hours before cooking, or even freeze them and cook from frozen, adding 3 or 4 minutes extra cooking time.

Most small filo parcels take relatively little time to cook and it is important to check them regularly towards the end of the cooking time, because they can literally pass from perfectly cooked and burnished golden brown to burnt and ruined in a matter of a couple of minutes.

Garlic: Wonderful, wonderful manna from heaven – without garlic, the cooking of the Mediterranean would stumble and fall, losing the breath that gives it life. Garlic is just essential and, what is more, it is amazingly good for you, a natural antiseptic that gives your insides a going over every time you eat it. It is practically the first thing you reach for when cooking any savoury recipe from anywhere around the Mediterranean. One of the finest (and most frequent) smells of the southern kitchen is that of garlic, and perhaps onions, sizzling in olive oil. Bliss. Olive oil and garlic ... a real marriage made in heaven. Together they form the basis for some of the most sensational sauces that light up simple, fresh foods. Think of *Aïoli* (see page 134), the Provençal butter, or in other words, garlic mayonnaise, or the powerhouse that is *Anchoïade* (see page 135), a blend largely of garlic, olive oil and anchovies.

When you are buying garlic, look for heads which are firm all over, and that smell of ... well, nothing very much at all. Funny that, isn't it? But there's a very good reason for it. You see, that garlicky smell which Britons used to be so scared of, but are now beginning to

drool over just like any red-blooded Spaniard, doesn't actually exist until the moment a garlic clove is cut into or damaged in some way. As the cell walls are breached, an almost instant chemical chain reaction occurs, creating that garlicky scent and releasing it into the air. Peel a clove and you can't help but damage it a little here and there, which will release a minor whiff. That's why dishes made with torrential quantities of whole garlic cloves don't blow your head off, as long as the garlic has been cooked, which halts the process. Sliced garlic will be more pungent, but not half as smelly as chopped garlic, and a mere pale echo of crushed garlic, which has by far the strongest smell and taste of all.

Lightly browned garlic is extremely good to eat (I love the taste of golden brown garlic 'crisps', in other words slices fried in olive oil, scattered over foods), but do take care not to overdo it. Dark brown or burnt garlic is bitter and quite disgusting and it doesn't take much to ruin a whole dish. Be warned.

Guanciale: Though *guanciale* is very similar to pancetta, it is actually made from pig's jowl, or 'cheek'. Like pancetta it has been salted and cured and, what's more, is used in similar ways. It is made in the Province of Lazio, around Rome, and is what should be used in *spaghetti alla carbonara* (with eggs) and *spaghetti all'amatriciana* (with tomato). I've rarely seen it for sale here, but pancetta makes a more than acceptable substitute.

Hallóumi: Hallóumi is a firm, almost rubbery, very salty cheese from Greece, often speckled with mint. I can't get enthusiastic about straight hallóumi, but it really comes into its own when it is fried or grilled (brush first with olive oil), since it holds its shape while softening and metamorphosing into something very good indeed. Serve it with a squeeze of lemon juice, and eat it while it is still hot.

Harissa: Moroccan harissa is hot, hot, hot. This thick spice paste, heavy with chillies, packs plenty of kick, so give it the kid-glove treatment until you get used to it. Underlying that pow! is a complex flavour (it also contains garlic, coriander and other spices and herbs), which makes it a first-class ingredient to stir into tomato sauces, or soups or stews for a quick pick-me-up, as long as you don't overdo it. It is often served as a condiment with a mound of couscous and its stew, to be added in greater or

lesser degree, according to the whim of each diner.

Herbes de Provence: This mix of herbs is what imbues so much of Provençal cooking with its characteristic sun-laden taste, and also, paradoxically, what may make the same dish differ from one establishment to another, and from summer to winter. How can that be? Easy – there is no hard and fast rule about the precise constituents of *herbes de Provence*, or the proportions in which they should be mixed. In the summer months the herbs may well be fresh, or a blend of fresh and dried, and in winter they will be dried which brings another dimension altogether. I've heard native cooks arguing about what should and shouldn't go into *herbes de Provence*, and if they can't agree, then how on earth can anyone pin down an exact recipe? No way am I going to risk life and limb by insisting on precise proportions of this and that.

The one thing I would add, before I give you a general idea of what could go into the mix, is that it really is worth buying small jars of genuine ready mixed *herbes de Provence* either when you are on holiday down in the South of France, or from good delis in this country. The pounding heat of high summer, and the aridity of the hills where many of the herbs are gathered from the wild, bequeaths a particular magic to their leaves. On top of that, the herbs chosen, for the most part, share one essential quality - their vivid aromatic flavour is intensified and enriched by drying.

Still, if you grow your own herbs, or want to capture something of that Provençal magic, here is a list of potential candidates for inclusion. Mix and match to your heart's desire.

rosemary
savory
wild thyme (or ordinary thyme in this
     country – lemon thyme is good too)
oregano
marjoram
hyssop
basil (fresh version only - dried basil is a
     waste of space)
bay
lavender flowers

Mix your chosen herbs together, crumbling larger ones such as rosemary or bay.

To use, add to meat stews, game, tomato dishes, braised vegetables, or rub into chicken, fish or chops before cooking with salt, pepper and olive oil (see *Barbecue Quails*, page 163).

Jamón Serrano: see Air-dried Hams.

Kaymak: *Kaymak* is an extra-thick clotted cream, made usually from water-buffalo milk, which is very rich. It is made from Greece, through Turkey and right round the Middle East (and even in Afghanistan). It is so thick that you can cut it with a knife. My first taste of the genuine article was in a dairy in the centre of Athens, where it was served with soft white rolls and Hymettus honey – the Greek equivalent of scones, clotted cream and strawberry jam. Indeed, clotted cream, though not quite so rich (hard to believe!) is an excellent substitute.

Kephalotiri: This hard Greek cheese is made from ewes' or goats' milk and has an excellent flavour, which can transform a humble moussaka into a real treat. It can be fried or grilled in fingers like hallóumi but the more mature cheese is usually grated. If you can't get it anywhere, use either a hard Italian pecorino, or a mixture of Parmesan and Gruyère – not that similar, it has to be said, but they taste good in their own way.

Lemons: This is the fruit that embodies the crystal-clear light of the Mediterranean. The brisk, sharp, yellow, waxy skin is pitted with tiny pockets, bulging with the perfume of the lemon zest, such a special flavour that takes its place so easily in sweet and savoury foods (think of grated lemon zest in *gremolata*, the Italian blend of finely chopped parsley, garlic and lemon zest sprinkled on to stews just before serving). Inside, the cargo of tart juice is the natural sharpening agent for anything from salad dressings to the coolest, most refreshing ices. An amazing, and utterly essential, fruit.

When buying lemons don't insist on a perfect symmetrical shape. A good lemon may be bumpy and uneven, with touches of green at the ends or here and there on the skin. What it should be is packed full, swollen with juice, inside a firm, taut skin that looks as if it is bursting with health (must be all that Vitamin C inside). Lemons are remarkably like humans in one thing – if their skin looks tired, dry and dull, then they are not at their best. Buy lemons that have not been waxed, especially if you are likely to use the zest. It's not

that the wax coating that most lemons get is going to poison you, but who wants to shove unnecessary chemicals down their friends' or family's throats? To get the maximum juice out of a lemon, warm it gently in a low oven, or in hot water, or even with a quick burst in the microwave, before squeezing.

Lemons, Preserved: These are Morocco's great contribution to the world of cooking. When lemons are preserved in salt and their own juice, a strange transformation occurs, softening the skin (it is this that is used, rather than the inner pulp), and giving it a unique flavour, scented but slightly (and pleasingly) polish-like. Sliced up finely, they make a striking addition to salads. It's not difficult to make your own (see page 132), certainly easier and probably quicker than tracking down the genuine article. I have bought them in the specialist section of one leading supermarket, and you may also find them in the occasional delicatessen.

Lentils: For a start you can forget all about yellow lentils and red lentils – they belong further afield. For Mediterranean-style salads and lentil stews you need small, whole green or brown lentils, the sort that will hold their shape when cooked.

There are three stars in the lentil firmament. The most renowned are Puy lentils from France, and they are quite honestly the most delicious lentils I have ever tasted. They are the most beautiful, tiny, slate grey and blue discs, grown in the Auvergne. The name is legally protected but even some reputable stores sell so-called Puy lentils that do not come from the right area, and do not even look like the genuine article. So, check the packet to make sure you are getting what you are paying for; if they come from France then they are probably the real McCoy, but if you find a little note saying 'Grown in Canada', or 'Product of Various Countries' or anything else along these lines be aware that although what you are getting may be very good, it is not the genuine article, so it should be priced accordingly.

From Italy, comes lentil star number two, the *lenticchie di Norcia*, on the small side again, this time brown rather than grey. Again, check claims boldly stated in large letters against the small print. Norcian lentils are less well known than Puy lentils so, if you do find some,

they are less likely to be pretenders. The same goes for fancy lentil number three, the larger brown Salamanca lentils, which are considered the very best by many Spaniards. In this country they are sold in smart delicatessens at an extortionate price and, I have to say, good though they were, I didn't feel that they quite justified such an enormous outlay.

When it comes to cooking lentils, there is absolutely no need to soak them. Rinsing, yes, but soaking, no. Pick over the lentils and remove any small stones or grit. Simmer in unsalted water or stock until they are tender – this may take as little as 15 minutes or a good deal longer, depending on age, size and variety. Keep checking, but don't undercook them – overly crisp, leguminous lentils are not too appealing, but then nor are mushy, fuzzy ones. Somewhere in between is what you are aiming for: a little firmer and nuttier for salads, a little softer and more comforting if served hot.

Mascarpone Cheese: As rich as Croesus, this is about as close to cream as a cheese can get. Heart-attack city here we come, but what a delightful way to go. Mascarpone is thick and unctuous, rich and silky smooth, a touch sweetish and devilishly delicious served with all kinds of puddings, instead of cream. To soften it a little, relaxing the texture a degree or two closer to a spooning cream, mix it with a few spoonfuls of milk or single cream. It gained fame on the back of tiramisu, of which it is a major component. Actually, I don't really like tiramisu that much, and I can think of a hundred and one ways of using mascarpone that are much more interesting. Have you ever tried it smeared thickly on meringues with a few fresh raspberries pressed into it? Divine. Or try using it instead of ordinary cream cheese in cheese cakes, or spoon a great big dollop into a pan of sautéd mushrooms to make a quick sauce, or in pasta, or in ice creams, or as a cake filling or with scones, and the list goes on.

One small piece of advice, learnt the hard way by yours truly. Don't try to make a tiramisu or anything that involves beating mascarpone with anything else on a very hot day, unless all your ingredients come straight from the fridge. In excessive heat, room-temperature mascarpone has an infuriating tendency to curdle.

Mint: Mint is an indispensable herb for summer eating, and makes regular appearances in Mediterranean food. Its revitalizing menthol freshness is its principal charm and, since this is largely destroyed by heat, there seems little point in cooking with it, apart from in a few very briefly cooked dishes. Use it in salads and dressings, or for making a refreshing infusion (see page 197) and don't be too stingy. If you want to grow your own, look for a variety called Moroccan Spearmint, which has a good, true flavour.

Mozzarella Cheese: Mozzarella is a *pasta filata* cheese; in other words, the curd is heated up until it becomes elastic and then wound up again to form balls. Well, anyone who has ever eaten a pizza knows how the mozzarella stretches into long, long threads. Most of what we get here is cows'-milk mozzarella, which is firmer and more rubbery than the traditional, gloriously tender, milky buffalo-milk mozzarella. These days, however, it is becoming increasingly easy to find buffalo mozzarella sold in sealed plastic bags in its own little pond of milky liquid. Sold like this, it is still not as good as a truly fresh one, but a vast improvement on the standard cows'-milk version. Eat buffalo mozzarella, sliced, with tomatoes and shavings of Parmesan for a quick first course.

Avoid the rectangular slabs of so-called mozzarella, whether they are made in Italy or elsewhere – the quality has been entirely sacrificed for the sake of convenience. Once the packet of mozzarella has been opened, the cheese can be kept, in a bowl in lightly salted water, for up to four days.

Olive Oil: Right around the rim of the Mediterranean sea, there are groves of grey-leaved olive trees, stacked in terraces up mountains or marching in neat ancient rows across the plains. The olive tree is virtually what defines the lands of the Mediterranean – it is certainly one of the things that links them all. Though the fruit of the tree is important, what matters most of all is the oil that is pressed from those fruit. To the Mediterranean cook, olive oil is commonplace, one of the fundamental,

totally essential cooking ingredients, yet it is rarely taken for granted. Talk to anyone from Spain, Italy, Egypt, Greece or the Lebanon about olive oil and they warm to the subject instantly, reminiscing about some olive grove they know well, recalling harvests and pressings, and tastings of the new oil, and good years and bad.

More northerly cooks, from the butter lands, may find this strange at first, but it doesn't take long to develop a taste for cooking with olive oil. Besides, it is indisputably good for you, reducing the harmful forms of cholesterol that may be rampaging around in your body, and encouraging the good forms.

For me, olive oil can be divided up into three broad categories. The cheapest olive oil, with the lightest flavour

(verging on negligible) is sold here simply as 'olive oil'. It is made by stripping all flavour from the rejected oils with chemicals and then replacing a modicum of taste with a slug or two of first-grade olive oil. It won't give you the real flavour of the Mediterranean. In fact it won't give you much flavour at all.

Then there are the blended, brand-name extra virgin olive oils. Legally, only the best quality oils can be labelled 'extra virgin' or, in other words, oils with less than 1% acidity and a fine flavour. Big brand-name oils will always taste the same, because they have been expertly blended to get the same balance every time. If you find one you particularly like, stick with it. These medium-price oils are just the ticket for everyday cooking.

Finally, there is the *crème de la crème*, or should that be '*huile de l'huile*'?

These are the single-estate extra virgin olive oils, the *grands crus* of the olive oil world. Using a wine term is not out of place, for olive oil is rather like wine. The flavour depends on many things – variety of olive, the stage of development at which it is picked, how it is picked, the terrain, the climate, and the season itself. Some years are better than others, and no two years will ever be quite the same, which means that these single-estate oils vary in taste from year to year. They are more costly, but they are produced with enormous care and attention to detail. Save them for dressing salads, or use as a condiment, drizzled over bread, or as the finishing touch to a soup or a hot dish of vegetables, meat or fish.

Unlike wine, olive oil does not keep. Don't lay down your best oils to mature; they'll just end up rancid. Enjoy them straight away and clear your shelves within the year, ready for the next season's extra virgin *nouveau*.

Olives: Heaven alone knows how anybody ever imagined that you could turn a raw olive into something that people would actually enjoy eating. I did once taste a ripe, raw olive and, believe me, it is downright disgusting. Still, luckily someone cracked it, somewhere along the line, and pickled cured olives are one of life's small pleasures. Of course, there are olives and olives, and they are not all worth consuming. I draw the line at pre-stoned olives, particularly of the black kind, which invariably taste soapy and miserable (they'd have been better left on the tree). If you are ever making something like tapenade, Provence's thick, black olive paste, it will taste vile if it's made with tinned ready-stoned olives. It's only worth doing if you take the time to stone whole olives one by one. Incidentally, there's a brilliant way of doing this that is at once fun, dramatic and effective. Place an olive on the work surface and then bash it hard with the back of a wooden spoon, splitting it open. The stone can now be easily eased out. Much more entertaining (and less wasteful) than a metal cherry or olive stoner. I do quite like the green olives stuffed with anchovies or almonds, but only as a nibble with drinks and definitely not for cooking with.

When you are travelling around the Mediterranean, take time to wander through the markets, where you are bound to find one or more olive stalls, selling oodles of different kinds of olives, black, green, purplish, small, middling, big, enormous, and all of them in endless different marinades with spices or chillies, or orange zest or herbs and so on. Try before you buy – this is standard practice.

The same advice goes back at home, if possible. If you are faced with a choice of only tins and jars, however, tasting will not be practical. In this case, good varieties to look out for are Gaeta, Kalamata, Niçoise and Picholine, amongst many others.

Orange Flower Water: The scent of orange blossoms is one of the most exquisite in the world. I can still remember the first time I smelled it, when I was fourteen, in the back streets of Famagusta in Cyprus – it made a huge impact on me then and I still adore it. Orange flower water captures that heavenly smell, ready to drip, drip, drip into sugar sweet pastries, and other puddings. It is also used in some savoury dishes – salads, and delicate stews, for instance – which takes a bit more getting used to. These days orange flower water can be bought not only in delicatessens but also in good supermarkets.

Oregano: Oregano is a rare thing, a herb that is actually better dried than it is fresh. There is some debate about the difference between marjoram and oregano (in fact they both share the Latin name *origanum*) but to me the main difference is that marjoram, with its warmth and sweetness, is better fresh, whilst the true delights of oregano only appear when it is dried. Custom has it, or rather had it, that oregano was the name for wild marjoram, though now commercial herb growers have muddied the issue by cultivating fresh oregano, which, may I say, is not much to write home about.

Anyway, I hope I haven't confused you, because when it comes down to the cooking of the Mediterranean, and in particular of Greece, Italy and Provence, the old definition still holds true. Thank heavens. The oregano that grows wild over arid hills in the stifling heat of the summer is something quite remarkable, its intense peppery flavour coming to the fore when it is dried. If you have a Greek or Italian deli near you, make a bee line for it and buy your dried oregano (the Greeks call it *rígani*) there for a taste of the real thing. Then you will understand why it is used with such abandon.

Paella Rice: see Rice.

Pancetta: Italian bacon, fair and square. Pancetta is salted and cured belly of pork. There are two main types of pancetta: *pancetta stesa* and *pancetta arrotolata*. *Pancetta stesa* is the simplest, plainest version, which may be used either thinly sliced, or diced to flavour sauces and stews, or wrapped around meat, vegetables or fish to slide on to skewers for kebabs. *Pancetta arrotolata* is seasoned with spices and then rolled up and cured. This type of pancetta is sometimes eaten raw, like prosciutto, as part of the *antipasti*, or first course. It can also be used in cooking, just like *pancetta stesa*. Either kind of pancetta may be smoked, in which case it is *pancetta affumicata*.

Pancetta is widely available now, though, infuriatingly, supermarkets often sell it only thinly sliced, when for many dishes it really needs to be diced. You can't have everything, I suppose.

Paprika: Paprika is the spice made by grinding dried paprika peppers to a powder. Now that sounds straightforward enough, but it isn't, because there are all sorts of very different paprikas to choose from, and my advice is to taste a little before using to make sure that you've got the right kind. Hungarian paprika is usually of high quality. The average consumption of paprika per person per annum in Hungary is a staggering 1 kg (2¼ lb), so they inevitably know a great deal about it. Their paprika, and most ordinary paprika produced elsewhere, is usually mild or 'sweet', but can also be hot, though not quite as hot as, say, cayenne pepper. The other major paprika-lovers are the Spanish but, in Spain, paprika can be quite a different affair. They transform paprika into one of the most exciting of spices, by smoking the peppers before grinding. Smoked sweet paprika brings a genuine smoky taste to foods and the good news is that it is now pretty easy to find in Britain. Look for it in supermarkets and shops that stock a good range of spices. Note that you can also get smoked hot paprika, as well as unsmoked Spanish paprika, mild or hot.

Paprika, Smoked: see Paprika.

Parma Ham: see Air-dried Hams.

Parmesan Cheese: This is the king of the cooking cheeses, and it is pretty damned fine as a table cheese, too. The making of Parmesan is strictly protected by law – it can only be made in a specific area around the northern Italian town of Parma, and no short cuts are allowed. It takes an incredible 16 litres (28 pints) of milk to make each kg (2¼ lb) of cheese. The huge truckle cheeses are aged for several years in vast warehouses kept at exactly the right temperature. Inspectors grade every cheese and give it their final stamp of approval (or not, in the case of inferior specimens) before it is allowed to sally forth under the famous name *Parmiggiano Reggiano*. Parmesan, or *parmiggiano*, is a *grano* cheese, or, in other words a hard, granular cheese, with the wonderful flavour packed into every tiny crumb.

Never waste your money on ready-grated Parmesan, unless it has been freshly grated that day at the deli counter and you intend to use it straight away. Most ready-grated Parmesan tastes pretty disgusting, and is a far, far cry from the genuine article.

Far better to buy a decent-sized hunk and grate it yourself as and when you need it. This means that you can also go for the frightfully fashionable shavings of Parmesan to strew over salads and pasta and all manner of other dishes. Use a vegetable peeler to scrape off paper-thin flakes of the cheese. Store unused Parmesan, wrapped in silver foil, in the fridge, making sure that you open it every day so that it can breathe.

Parsley: We're talking flatleaf parsley here, rather than the more northerly curly-leaf variety, though in fact, when it comes down to it, there is precious little difference in flavour (if you don't believe me, try chopping a few leaves of both up very finely, so that no one can tell which is which from the texture, and then do a few blind tastings). But for authenticity's sake, and since flatleaf parsley is easy enough to buy (or grow) these days, opt for the flatleaf version when you are cooking Mediterranean food. Parsley is of major importance right around the Med, just as crucial as some of the more glamorous hot-weather herbs such as coriander or basil. I think that they also appreciate it far more, using it not just as a background flavour or a garnish but also as an important ingredient in sauces like *Salsa Verde* (see page 127), or in the herb salads of North Africa.

Like coriander leaf, for the best value and often the best quality flatleaf parsley, you will need to make a trip to an ethnic food shop, where it is usually sold in huge, happy bunches. If you are not using it all immediately, wrap in kitchen towel wrung out in cold water, inside a plastic bag, in the vegetable drawer of the fridge. When the supermarket is the only option, ignore their pots of too-tightly-packed, weedy flatleaf parsley, with no flavour and no substance, and stick with the teensy plastic packs. Incidentally, on average I reckon that the contents of 2–3 of those constitutes what I would call a bunch.

Passata: see Tomatoes.

Pasta There can be few people in this country, or indeed in most of Europe, who have not eaten pasta in one of its many and varied forms. And heaven knows how we non-Italian mothers ever kept our children happily fed before we became acquainted with pasta – I know that my children would easily live on it and precious little else. The wonderful neutrality of pasta means that it can be dressed with an infinite number of sauces, from the simplest *aglio e olio* – olive oil, garlic and freshly grated Parmesan – to any number of fancy creations with caviare, lobster or truffles.

But back to basics. Pasta at its plainest is a flour and water dough, and at its best is a mixture of durum flour (very hard wheat flour) and eggs. In Italy, most households, most of the time, will be perfectly content with dried pasta straight from the packet. They do not consider that fresh pasta is necessarily any better, except perhaps when the women of the family get together to roll and stretch their own home-made pasta for a special family meal. So, don't you go believing that fresh shop-bought pasta in a clear container is inevitably superior to something out of a packet. It's one and only guaranteed advantage is that it is phenomenally quick to cook, but let's face it, 8–10 minutes, the time it takes for many dried pastas to cook, is hardly excrutiatingly drawn-out.

There are a few basic rules to cooking pasta. The first is that you should use an enormous saucepan – the largest you have, probably. The second is to add plenty of salt to the water and this is where many non-Italians go wrong. The Italian food writer Anna del Conte reckons that you should add 100 g (3½ oz) salt to every litre (1¾ pints) of water. This is far, far more than most of us ever chuck in, but if you are bold enough to do it, I guarantee your pasta will taste 10 times better. Don't add any oil to the water – it's not necessary. Make sure that the water is at a rolling boil before adding the pasta, and bring it back to a rolling boil as soon as you can. Allow 3–4 oz (90–110 g) pasta per person, unless they have gargantuan appetites. Cook the pasta until al dente, or in other words, tender, but still with a slight resistance to the bite. Have the sauce ready and waiting by this stage. Drain the pasta, but not too thoroughly, and then dress immediately with the sauce before the individual strands or shapes start to glue together. If your pasta has been beautifully cooked, in well-salted water, you will find that you need relatively little of a good sauce with a deep flavour, to dress the pasta.

Although it is entirely up to you which shape pasta you marry with which sauce, there are some basic guidelines to make choices easier. Spaghetti is best suited to light sauces based largely on olive oil, and to good tomato based sauces. Wider ribbons of pasta of one sort or another, are perfect for creamier sauces, or sauces based on eggs, meat or cheese. Cups and shells and similar sorts of pasta shapes are excellent for bitty sauces, because each little dimple and hollow will trap small chunks of this or that. Middling sized tubular pasta, such as elbow macaroni, is often matched with sauces that contain pulses. For baked pasta dishes, there are either the flat sheets of lasagne, or chunky tubular forms such as penne.

Pastry, Filo: see Filo Pastry.

Pecorino: Pecorino is the Italian for sheep's-milk cheese, and there are many different kinds of pecorino to choose from. Usually when recipes call merely for 'pecorino' (particularly if it is to be grated or shaved into flakes), they mean one of the matured, hard pecorinos. The most famous of these are the *pecorino romano* (from the area around Rome) and *pecorino siciliano* (from Sicily) which are both as hard as Parmesan and pack in an intense flavour – try making a pesto with either of these, or grating them over pasta.

There are also softer pecorinos, such as the wonderful *pecorino toscano* (from Tuscany), which is superb with ripe pears, a classic way to end a Tuscan meal, but which I've also eaten as a first course, with shavings of truffles and fine olive oil. You'll only come across these pecorinos in very good cheese shops, or in situ in Tuscany or in Sardinia, where they also make a superb soft pecorino.

Peppers: It takes a trip to Spain or Italy to discover how special sweet red and green, especially green, peppers can really taste. Back home, we have to settle most of the time for the perfectly pleasant uniform little boxes, that stack and pack so very neatly, with their glossy mono-colour skins. Matters may just be beginning to move on, however. I've noticed, here and there, sneaking on to shelves, peppers that look rather more like the peppers of a continental market. Longer, not so perfectly and evenly coloured, with twisted uneven forms that are fascinating to gaze upon. They are blessed with a mite more flavour and individuality, too. Look out for them.

Raw peppers are okay, but they are rarely served like this in the Mediterranean, for the simple reason, I suspect, that they taste so very much better when they have been cooked. Heat really brings out the complex nature that is missing in uncooked peppers (true even for our perfect little boxes). Peppers may be fried, or sweated, but the best way of all to cook them is to grill or barbecue them. Either way, make sure that the heat is at maximum force and then arrange the peppers fairly close to the grill. Grill or barbecue, turning every now and then, until they are, quite literally, blackened and blistered all over. Pop them into a plastic bag, and knot loosely. Leave to cool and then just pull the skins away from the tender flesh and cut away stem and seeds. What a transformation! Grilled peppers have a hundred and one uses, but the most obvious is as a salad. Dress with extra virgin olive oil, a touch of balsamic vinegar, crushed garlic if you wish, salt and pepper, and there it is, one of the all-time-great salads.

Pine Nuts: Pine nuts or pine kernels are extracted from the cones of the magnificent Stone pine that one sees so often around the shores of the Mediterranean sea (though an awful lot of the pine nuts sold in big stores here come from China). The pine cones are harvested in the autumn, stored until summer and then dried in the hot sun. The individual pine nuts will then drop out, still sheathed in a brittle case. This case is the reason why pine nuts are so expensive, since each tiny nut has to be extracted without breaking it. I've bought the nuts, still in their cases, from Asian shops, and have passed them around with drinks, rather like peanuts or shell-on pistachios. Their flavour has been superb, but I really couldn't face the thought of shelling enough at any one time to use in cooking.

The quality of shelled pine nuts varies enormously. I've recently bought some that were horribly mealy and dull in flavour, whereas they should be sweet and buttery, and, if you are really lucky, still with a hint of that resinous scent one associates with pine trees. Though they are widely available, the very best shelled pine nuts that I have ever bought have always come from Middle Eastern groceries, grown usually in the Lebanon.

Pine nuts do not have a long shelf life because of their high oil content. Once a packet has been opened, store them in the fridge and use up quickly. Lightly toasted or fried, they make a delicious addition to salads, and are fantastic scattered over thick Greek yoghurt, drizzled with honey and a little orange flower water.

Pistachio Nuts: The small pistachio tree just loves the heat and grows in the most unpropitious locations, clinging on to rocky hillsides where little else will thrive. Not surprising then, that it has made itself firmly at home in northern Africa and the Middle East, where pistachio nuts are eaten with gay abandon. Ash trays piled high with their hard shells are much in evidence of an evening, after long sessions shelling pistachios and enjoying their salted green flesh. They appear in many syrup-sticky pastries, more for their colour, on the whole, than their flavour. In Italy they make a striking appearance in the form of green pistachio ice-cream, or dotted through mortadella, that enormous pork sausage.

For cooking, check that the nuts have not been salted before buying. For a true unmuddied green colour, skin the pistachios by covering them with boiling water, leaving for about 1 minute and then draining them and slipping out of their skins.

Pomegranate Syrup: This is the concentrated juice of a variety of sour pomegranate, with a thick, velvety texture and a dark brown colour. It is fabulous stuff, particularly well suited to dressing salads such as *Bazargan* (see page 48). The flavour is tart and fruity and utterly unlike that of vinegar or even lemon juice. It is also used in stews and soups, imparting its own unique tang. I like it, too, with fish.

Pomegranates: The clear, pink juicy seeds of the pomegranate are beautiful to behold. Piled up high, in a pretty bowl, they glitter and glimmer like precious jewels. Extracting them, on the other hand, is a slow job as they have to be assiduously separated from the bitter white membrane they cling to. Unless you have a flock of children or servants, it will take you an age to prepare enough of the seeds to make a mound of any significance. Better to use the seeds as a garnish scattered over a fruit salad or a creamy pudding, or over the small savoury salads that grace the tables of North Africa and the Middle East. To squeeze the juice, treat the pomegranates like citrus fruit, halving them and squeezing out the juice on a citrus squeezer.

Porcini: *Porcini* is the Italian for both 'little pig' and for cep mushrooms. Cep are the classiest of all wild mushrooms, chunky, meaty and oozing character. Italians are big wild-mushroom gatherers, like the French, and this is one of their major prizes. For those who don't have the knack, the knowledge or the time, autumnal markets are piled high with these gems.

Many are also dried, and this is the easiest way to get your hands on this big, big flavour back home at any time of the year. Dried porcini may seem expensive but, trust me, you only need a few grams to make a major impact. To use, rehydrate by soaking in warm water, or in sherry or other alcohol for about 30 minutes until soft and floppy. Pick out the mushrooms and then leave the soaking liquid to settle. Pour it off carefully so as not to disturb the woodland grit that will have settled at the bottom. If you aren't using this mushroomy liquor in the recipe, freeze it to use in a mushroom sauce or soup. The soaked mushrooms can be added to stuffings, sauces, stews, or just simple cultivated mushroom fry-ups with lots of garlic, please, and perhaps a slug of white wine (see page 35).

Preserved Lemons: see Lemons, Preserved.

Prosciutto: see Air-dried Hams.

Rice: Rice was first cultivated in Asia many millennia ago, but it is a relatively recent arrival around the Mediterranean. It was first grown in Egypt nearly two and a half thousand years ago and eventually the Moors took it with them as their armies marched on Spain and Italy. Now it is an important staple in most Mediterranean countries, widely grown wherever there is plentiful water to feed its thirst. New varieties have been developed over the centuries and from these come specific dishes, which take advantage of the characteristics of locally grown rice.

Risotto rice, grown around the Po Valley in Italy, has short, stubby grains that absorb enormous amounts of liquid without collapsing to a mush. It is also very starchy, which is what gives a risotto its creamy consistency. The most widely sold type of risotto rice is *arborio*, but the best of all in my book is the rarer *vialone nano*, which you may be able to buy in Italian delicatessens. *Carnaroli* is also very good.

From the swampy area near Valencia in Spain comes paella rice, or Valencia rice, which, like risotto rice, has a short, stubby grain and absorbs a good quantity of liquid, though it isn't as starchy and is usually washed before use. If you have the choice, buy *categoria extra* Spanish rice, which will have a minimum of 95% whole grains (too many broken grains make for a mushy dish). Spanish rice is available from some large supermarkets and Spanish delicatessens. Spanish rice dishes should always be cooked in shallow, wide dishes because the grains are particularly tender, and more likely to be crushed to a sticky mass in a narrower saucepan.

For pilaus or pilafs, the ideal rice comes from Iran, which you may be able to track down in Middle Eastern food stores. In fact, I usually use a long-grain rice, either American or, better still, Indian basmati rice, which has the finest flavour of all long grains, and invariably keeps its shape when cooked.

Ricotta Cheese: *Ricotta* literally means 're-cooked', which is exactly how this soft, creamy cheese is made. It is technically a by-product of cheese making – the first 'cooking' comes when the milk for the main cheese is warmed through, allowing the whey to separate from the curds. Ricotta is then made by heating the whey again, until curds of ricotta form on the top. Ricotta cheese has a mild, milky, cool, fresh flavour and must be used and eaten soon after it has been made or, in our more modern world of supermarkets and the like, soon after the tub has been opened. It makes the basis of many Italian baked cheesecakes, and is often used in stuffings for ravioli and other pasta shapes. Italian pastry-makers use it in

fillings for all manner of sweet pastries and tarts, or it can simply be mixed with diced chocolate, candied peel, coffee, and/or rum and the like to make a simple creamy pudding on its own (see page 192).

You can also buy a smoked ricotta from Sicily, or the salty, mature *ricotta salata*, a firm cheese for cooking with.

Rígani: see Oregano.

Risotto Rice: see Rice.

Rocket: Rocket has been the designer salad leaf here for well over a decade now, so it looks like it's here to stay. Hip hip hooray! I love the stuff with its energetic peppery kick. Naturally, there are several different forms of rocket – petite tender leaves known as roquette, jagged wild rocket with a big punch, plain, medium-sized, strong but not too strong rocket, and *rokka*, big leaved, mature rocket sold very cheaply in Greek and Turkish food stores, perfect for cooking, but perhaps a bit over the top for salads. In Italy it may be called *arugula* or *rucola*, depending on where you are, and not only is it included in salads, but it also goes into wild leaf mixes for stuffings.

Modern Mediterranean cooking is largely founded on a bed of rocket. It slips nicely and comfortably under slabs of grilled tuna, char-grilled chicken, pan-fried prawns and so on, which is fine by me. A handful of rocket is an easy and pleasing way to dress up a plateful of food, and it is rarely superfluous. Lovely stuff, so keep it coming!

Rosemary: A herb that is much favoured in both Italian and French cooking. It is powerful, so needs to be used with some care, though, having said that, I think we are far too cautious with it here. The Italians have no qualms about using it with abundance, where the dish can take it, often chopping the tough leaves up very finely so that they can be eaten with ease. The superb *Arista alla Fiorentina* (see page 152) is stuffed full of rosemary, and yet, when it has been cooked, the meat is not overwhelmed but greatly enhanced. More surprising than meat with rosemary are both fish and vegetables with rosemary. Red mullet with rosemary (lots of it, again finely chopped) is a blissful combination, while roast potatoes, or roast red onions and carrots are vastly improved by adding several generous branches of rosemary.

When I say rosemary, I mean fresh rosemary not dried, which is quite another matter. The dried stuff is prickly, painful and horribly camphorous. Since rosemary grows easily, and is available all year round from shops, there really is no excuse for not using the fresh leaves all the time. If you do grow it, don't waste the trimmings when you cut it back – they make very good skewers for tender meats and fish, imparting their flavour from the inside out.

Rose Water: This is the diluted essence of scented rose petals – a truly romantic ingredient, that is used in delicate puddings to impart a wistful, old-fashioned fragrance. It's not to everyone's liking (my husband once described a dish I'd made with rose water in it as tasting 'like a tart's boudoir'), but when it is used subtly, it can lift, say, a simple dish of strawberries right out of the ordinary. It needs a little sugar (or more depending on the dish) to bring it to life. It is good in milky puddings, delicate creams and bavarois, or with fruit. Not so long ago, you could only buy it in chemists, but now it is sold by larger supermarkets and many delicatessens.

Saffron: The spice of kings and aristocracy, saffron is more expensive gram per gram than gold. But there's no need to pay a king's ransom for it, since all you need is a good pinch, a mere fraction of a gram, to bring its strange almost metallic tones to the average panful of rice or tomato sauce. It famously brings with it the colour of primroses and gold, with tell-tale streaks of orange red, but be suspicious of any dish that purports to be flavoured with saffron and is a brilliant canary yellow. To get that depth of colour you would need so much saffron that not only would it push up the price way out of reach, but it would also be quite unpalatable. The colour is fake, for saffron is a prime example of 'too much of a good thing is worse than none at all'.

Saffron is best bought whole, in a tangle of rich red threads, the dried style branches and stigma (usually referred to as the stamens, in a most unbotanical way) of the purple saffron crocus. You can use the threads whole or ground. To grind, first dry-fry them for a matter of 5 seconds or so in a pan over a hot heat, to crisp them up, and then grind to a powder in a mortar. Before using the threads, soak them in hot water or milk for at least 15 minutes. Ready-ground saffron can usually be added straight to the dish being cooked. Either way, add saffron later rather than earlier, so that the full entrancing flavour is preserved. Obviously, in cakes and breads the saffron will have to be baked in from the beginning but the moist dough is enough to protect it.

Sage: It is easy to think of sage as a particularly British herb, much in evidence in stuffings and sausages, but it is also a considerable favourite in Italy, where they use it with rather more panache. Here it is threaded on to skewers between chunks of meat or fish, so that its scent sinks into the flesh as they cook together; it perfumes butters for dressing pasta; and it is frizzled in hot oil to bring a new note to a tomato sauce. It goes with meat, naturally, but I think of it more in conjunction with veal than pork in Italy. Anyway, the thing is that sage is a truly glamorous herb when used well, but dried sage is an abomination. If you have any lurking on your shelves, chuck it out before you are tempted to use it. No self-respecting Italian cook would substitute dried sage for fresh – he or she would know that this musty, dusty, shrivelled shadow of its former self is not to be commended.

Sherry Vinegar: see Vinegar.

Smoked Paprika: see Paprika.

Sumac: There's many a sumac tree growing in gardens around this country, with furry-looking brick-red fruit. These are the cousins, usually poisonous, of the Elm-Leaved or Sicilian Sumac, from which comes the spice sumac, much used in Middle Eastern cooking. Sumac the spice is rather remarkable. It is a crystalline brick-red powder, with an enticingly sour taste to it. It is in effect a condiment, often sprinkled over grilled meats and fish, stirred into yoghurt with herbs as a relish, or shaken over salads to bring a sharp note to the greenery. It is to be found in Middle Eastern groceries, has a fairly lengthy shelf life and is well worth buying if you are keen on barbecues and al fresco eating.

Sun-dried Tomatoes: see Tomatoes.

Taleggio: An Italian cheese from melting heaven. It comes from the foothills of the Alps, a soft, high-butter-fat cheese with a mild taste. Try laying slices of it over cooked sliced new potatoes and flashing them under the grill for a few minutes. The result is a dish of gluttonous decadence that you may want to keep all for yourself. I've used it frequently on pizzas, where it is reduced by the heat of the oven to a molten pool. It is also excellent tossed into very hot pasta. Add cubes of mozzarella, dolcelatte or Gorgonzola, and shavings of Parmesan and you have *pasta ai quattro formaggi*, or, more prosaically, pasta with four cheeses. Mmmmm. Taleggio is sold in some of the larger supermarkets, and by good delicatessens. If you can't get it, a spoonful of mascarpone on a pizza or pasta makes up to some degree for the disappointment.

Tomatoes: It has become a bit of a cliché to complain about how poor tomatoes are here, and how wonderful they are in the Mediterranean. Unfortunately, like so many clichés, it's true to a certain extent. I say to a certain extent, because things are changing slowly, and because there are always exceptions to every cliché. At least we have a choice here and, if we want to spend more on tomatoes 'grown for flavour' (Q. What else would you grow them for? A. Profit and the retailer's convenience. Ha, ha, ha.) we can. They do taste better, but I have rarely, if ever, tasted a bought tomato in this country that could compare with a tomato picked straight from the plant in our garden in the late summer, or, more to the point, with a fully ripened Mediterranean tomato in high summer. That is the perfect tomato, sweet, sharp and so inspiringly, purely tomatoey that you could shout for joy.

The point is, though, that throughout eight or nine months of the year, the tomatoes sold in the Mediterranean, even in the best markets, are not much better than the best of ours. And that is why wise housewives in Italy and Spain lay down the best of the crop for use throughout the rest of the year, in the form of bottled, sieved tomato sauce (passata), as thick, semi-dried tomato purée, and here and there, though not as much as we might imagine, as sun-dried tomatoes. Nor, for that matter, are tinned tomatoes looked down upon. Obviously, you wouldn't serve them straight from the tin, just warmed through (yuck), but for sauces and soups and stews, cooked down slowly and at length with other ingredients, they are infinitely better than out-of-season hot-house tomatoes.

If you do want to cook with fresh tomatoes, the best way to imitate the very choicest, ripe tomatoes is to season duller fresh tomatoes with a touch of sugar and, perhaps also, a drop or two of vinegar if they are on the bland side. If they are being cooked, a tablespoon or so of tomato purée will bring depth to their dullness. Alternatively, use sugary little cherry tomatoes where appropriate – in salads for instance, but obviously not in sauces where you need to peel and seed them before cooking!

You do see sun-dried tomatoes down in the south of Italy, but I think it is fair to say that overall, they are less popular in Italy than they are here. Who cares? They taste so good, that I don't care one jot if they are not everyday fare elsewhere. With their intense caramel flavour, they add a special touch to dishes of pasta, or to sandwiches or even a simple *anti pasto* of cured meats and cheeses.

Vinegar: Good vinegar, like good oil, makes all the difference, not just to a salad, though that is where it is most obvious, but to all sorts of other dishes, where a dash of sharpness can harmonize the flavours. In the non-Muslim Mediterranean countries, vinegar almost always means wine vinegar. In Muslim countries, vinegar is unknown as alcohol is prohibited. No alcohol means no vinegar (the word literally means 'sour wine'), so other souring agents such as lemon juice, tamarind, pomegranate syrup, sumac and so on, take its place.

It is worth trekking off to a good delicatessen to buy your wine vinegar. Search out a really classy affair. It will cost a bit more but it's not as if you regularly use vinegar in vast quantities. One bottle should last a fair while. By classy, I mean a vinegar made from good-quality wine (cheap, gut-rot wine will produce cheap, gut-rot vinegar), by the slow Orleans method, or in other words by mixing wine and vinegar in barrels, inoculating it with a mother of vinegar (a naturally occurring, non-toxic spread of bacteria that floats on the surface), and leaving it in open barrels to turn slowly, slowly into vinegar. This way, all the finest qualities and nuances of the wine are preserved, resulting in a top-notch vinegar. Cheap wine vinegars are much quicker to produce, get heated up in the process, and lose most of the subtler flavours on the way. Red wine vinegar tends to be fuller bodied than white but, again, that depends enormously on the wine it has been made from. A really big, butch, bold white wine will produce a big, butch, bold white wine vinegar.

One of the most reliable and aromatic of wine vinegars is sherry vinegar, which, at its best, is a match for the more renowned balsamic vinegar. Good sherry vinegar has the enormous subtlety and depth that come direct from the characteristics of good sherry. I've found that sherry vinegar withstands heat better than most wine vinegars and, more particularly, balsamic vinegar so, if you are looking for a vinegar to drizzle into a hot sauce or stew, this is one of your best bets.

Balsamic vinegar hit the food-fashion headlines in the eighties, the ultimate in food snobbery. It is not technically a wine vinegar since it is made from the cooked must (juice) of the Trebbiano and other grapes. Balsamic vinegar comes from Modena and the surrounding area, where it is greatly treasured. Over many years, the vinegar is matured, in a sequence of barrels made of different woods (oak, ash, juniper, chestnut, cherry, mulberry and so on), becoming increasingly syrupy and rich and condensed, gathering an orchestra of different notes from each of the successive woods it meets, sweet, sour, aromatic and defying description. I've tasted balsamic vinegars up to 40 years old, and believe me they get better and better. Really ancient vinegar, 100 years or more old, must be out of this world, but then so is the price.

The cheapest balsamic vinegars are not particularly old, and have yet to gain the exquisite taste and consistency of a truly good, mature vinegar. Still, they are not bad at all, and make a welcome contribution to salads and sauces. But move on to the teenagers, some 8 to 12 years old, and the change is dramatic. These really are worth shelling out for, and they are not prohibitively expensive, considering that a mere half teaspoon or so over steamed vegetables, or a small tomato salad is all that you really need. Don't heat good-quality balsamic vinegars – you'll spoil them. However, for a crude approximation of a teenager, you can boil down cheap balsamic vinegar until it is reduced to a syrupy consistency. There's little to lose and a worthwhile amount to gain.

Vinegar, by the way, keeps almost indefinitely, in a well sealed bottle, away from direct sunlight.

COOK'S NOTES

One of the best things about cooking Mediterranean food is the freedom. A handful of this, a handful of that, a bunch of this herb, half a bunch of another. 'Please yourself' is the main tenet, trust your sense of taste; make something that you really like and it's pretty likely that other people will like it too. Mediterranean cooking is about making the most of what is available, not about dictatorial rules and precise measurements – after all, no two tomatoes are alike, and the olive oil produced from olive groves that face each other across a valley will never taste exactly the same, let alone the olive oil from two different countries, hundreds of miles apart.

All the recipes in this book have been tested in my home kitchen, not in some perfect, scientifically controlled laboratory of a kitchen. I have been as precise in specifying quantities as I can be, but don't hesitate to adjust the seasonings and so on to suit you and the ingredients themselves. It is customary to state at the front of cookery books that you should use either the metric measurements or the imperial ones, but not a mixture of the two. Well, with this sort of cooking I can't see that mixing and matching makes an enormous difference, with the minor exceptions of cakes, sauces based on eggs and a few puddings. Still, most of us are more comfortable thinking either in pounds and ounces, or in kilos and grammes, so stick with whichever set of measurements you feel most at home with. And that's fine, too.

There are, however, a few particulars of the way I work that may be helpful when you are using these recipes. I always use large eggs, unless otherwise stated, and, for preference, free-range eggs. All spoon measurements are rounded, unless otherwise stated. I use a 5 ml teaspoon and a 15 ml tablespoon. Every last drop of olive oil is extra virgin olive oil. For day-to-day cooking, I use a good brand of blended extra virgin olive oil and, for salads and as a condiment, I will use a more expensive, more individual, single-estate olive oil. Neither of these things is obligatory but, if you substitute what is sold as plain 'olive oil' for the extra virgin you will lose out considerably on flavour. If money is no object (lucky you!) you could use single-estate olive oils and nothing less all of the time.

I love using fresh herbs; they really do have by far the better, livelier flavour, which is exactly what makes Mediterranean cooking so good. There is a major and a minor exception to this rule: oregano is the major one, since dried oregano is so much more interesting than fresh; and bay leaf is the minor one, since bay leaves are, I find, marginally better dried than fresh. For most cooking purposes I use coarse Maldon salt or French grey coarse sea salt, although there are some instances where a fine-ground salt is more useful. Pepper is always black and freshly ground, and nutmeg, too, must be freshly grated.

To sterilize jars, wash them in soapy water, then rinse well. Turn the jars upside down on a wire rack in a low oven to dry (around 100°C/200°F/Gas Mark ½), without touching the insides. Leave for at least half an hour, and use straight from the oven. If you need cold sterilized jars, take them out of the oven and leave to cool, upside down, taking great care not to touch the insides. Fill quickly before sneaky bacteria and moulds get a chance to slide in.

Treat cooking times as approximate guidelines, and not as rules set in stone. Most oven manufacturers allow for an extraordinary 10% variation in oven temperature, which means that, if you set your oven for, say, 200°C/400°F/Gas Mark 6, you could actually be cooking at a temperature anywhere between 220°C/450°F/Gas Mark 7 and 180°C/350°F/Gas Mark 4. The answer is to check things as they cook, letting your senses – sight, smell, taste, touch and yes, even hearing – tell you when something is done and ready to eat.

CHAPTER ONE

STARTERS & SNACKS

AÏGO BOULIDO

GARLIC BROTH

In Provence they say that '*aïgo boulido sauvo la vido*', which translates literally as 'garlic broth saves your life'. In other words, this is a soup for the day after the night before. Both garlic and sage are considered cures for over-indulgence and, combined in this soothing but invigorating soup, they are meant to do wonders for a hangover or indigestion. It is also an excellent, light way to launch a supper party with a rich main course and big pudding.

Though a full ten garlic cloves are simmered in the pan, the broth itself is not overly garlicky. If you are particularly partial to the taste of raw garlic, rub the bread with a cut clove to build a kick-start into the cure. I love the austerity of the soup when it is made with plain tap water but, for dinner parties and the like, use good-quality, home-made stock to give it a more complex flavour (but not stock cubes or the like, which would ruin it).

SERVES 4

10 garlic cloves
6 fresh sage leaves
1 bay leaf
1 generous fresh thyme sprig
2 tablespoons extra virgin olive oil, plus extra
   for serving
1 litre (1¾ pints) water or light chicken stock
3 egg yolks, beaten
salt and freshly ground black pepper

TO SERVE:

8 slices baguette, toasted
1 halved garlic clove (optional)
grated Gruyère cheese

Crush each whole garlic clove roughly with the flat of a knife, leaving it more or less in one piece but squashed flat, then peel (you'll find the skin comes off incredibly easily). Put the peeled, squashed garlic cloves into a saucepan with the sage, bay, thyme, olive oil, water or stock and salt and pepper. Bring up to the boil and simmer gently for 15 minutes. While it cooks, rub one side of each piece of toast with the cut garlic clove, if using, and place two in each bowl. Drizzle a little extra olive oil over each one.

Once the soup has simmered for quarter of an hour, pick out and discard the bay leaf and thyme (but not the sage) and turn off the heat. Whisk 3 tablespoons of the hot soup into the eggs, then tip the whole lot back into the saucepan and stir. Taste and adjust the seasoning. Pour the soup into a hot tureen to serve. At the table, ladle the *aïgo boulido* into the bowls, set before the diners, and pass the Gruyère separately.

GAZPACHO

After paella, this must be the best-known of all Spanish recipes and, when it is made with good tomatoes, it is the perfect iced soup for a hot summer's day. And there's the rub. Though you can fiddle and play around adding this and that, there really is no substitute for ripe, fragrant, sweet yet slightly sharp, sun-ripened tomatoes. Gazpacho is only worth making if you can pull the tomatoes fully ripe straight from the plant, or if you are lucky enough to lay your hands on exceptionally good shop- or market-bought fruit. Save it for those special occasions, and it will remain the triumph that it should be.

SERVES 6

750 g (1½ lb) ripe, richly flavoured tomatoes, skinned, seeded and roughly chopped
¾ cucumber, peeled and roughly chopped
1 large green pepper, seeded and roughly chopped
2 garlic cloves, roughly chopped (optional)
½ red onion, chopped
2–2½ tablespoons red wine vinegar or sherry vinegar
100 g (4 oz) fresh white breadcrumbs
150 ml (5 fl oz) tomato juice
4 tablespoons extra virgin olive oil
½–1 teaspoon sugar
salt and freshly ground black pepper

TO SERVE – ANY OR ALL OF THE FOLLOWING:

tomatoes, skinned, seeded and diced
cucumber, diced
red onion, diced
green pepper, seeded and diced
***jamón serrano*, diced**
hard-boiled egg, shelled and chopped

Mix all the vegetables, the vinegar and the breadcrumbs. Place a quarter of the mixture in the liquidizer with the tomato juice, 1 tablespoon of olive oil, salt, pepper, a pinch or two of sugar and a slurp of iced water if necessary. Liquidize until smooth, then repeat with the remaining ingredients, each time adding about 150 ml (5 fl oz) of icy cold water instead of the tomato juice. Mix the whole lot together, then taste and adjust the seasoning, adding a little more salt, vinegar or sugar as necessary to highlight the flavours.

Chill, and adjust the seasoning again just before serving. Place all the garnishes in small bowls and pass around for people to help themselves.

SALMOREJO
TOMATO AND GARLIC CREAM

Salmorejo and gazpacho are kissing cousins, born out of frugality and an abundance of scarlet tomatoes, fruity olive oil and yesterday's bread. *Salmorejo*, however, is not a soup. It should be thick enough to eat with a fork (though with our rather insipid tomatoes I found I had to use more, which made my *salmorejo* sloppier), or at least to spoon on to a plate without courting disaster. A drizzle of olive oil and slices of cool vegetables and salty ham transform the salmon pink purée into a filling first course or even a main course of beautiful simplicity.

Adding egg yolks makes it a more luxurious dish, but they are by no means necessary if you are concerned about eating raw egg. *Piquillo* peppers are small, red peppers that are grilled and skinned by hand, then preserved in jars or tins. Some supermarkets and delicatessens sell them over here, but you could substitute strips of home-grilled and skinned red peppers.

SERVES 4–6
500 g (1 lb 2 oz) sturdy bread, crusts removed
500 g (1 lb 2 oz) well flavoured, scarlet, ripe
  tomatoes, skinned, seeded and roughly chopped
3 garlic cloves, chopped
2 egg yolks (optional)
1 tablespoon sherry vinegar
1–2 tablespoons tomato purée
125–150 ml (4–5 fl oz) extra virgin olive oil
salt and freshly ground black pepper

TO SERVE:
4–6 tablespoons extra virgin olive oil
4 slices *jamón serrano*, cut into strips
½ cucumber, peeled and sliced about 3 mm
  (⅛ inch) thick
1 hard-boiled egg, shelled and chopped
1 *piquillo* pepper, cut into strips
6 radishes, sliced
½ green pepper, seeded and diced
***picos* (short Spanish breadsticks) or long breadsticks**

Tear the bread up into small pieces and place in a bowl. Cover with cold water and leave for 10 minutes to soften. Drain, then squeeze out the water firmly with your hands. Put the bread in the processor with the tomatoes, garlic, egg yolks if using, vinegar, tomato purée, salt and pepper. Process to a smooth paste, gradually trickling in the oil. Taste and adjust the seasoning. Chill the purée, covered, until almost ready to eat. Bring back to room temperature (unless it's high summer and you need something cooling).

Divide the mixture between four or six shallow soup bowls or plates. Spoon 1 tablespoon of olive oil around each heap, then scatter with a mixture of some or all of the garnishes. Serve with *picos* or breadsticks.

ZUPPA DI VERDURA
BEAN AND VEGETABLE SOUP

This big, warming vegetable soup comes from Tuscany, where soups rather than pasta are the preferred first course. They have a tendency to be very substantial, leaving room for just a small main course to follow. For a light lunch or supper, I'd be quite happy with a bowl of *zuppa di verdura*, followed by fruit and cheese.

If you are short of time, you can substitute 400 g (14 oz) drained, tinned cannellini beans for the dried ones, but you lose a little of the flavour given by the beans' cooking water.

SERVES 6

1 fresh rosemary sprig

1 generous fresh thyme sprig

2 bay leaves

200 g (7 oz) dried cannellini or haricot beans, soaked overnight

4 tablespoons extra virgin olive oil

1 onion, chopped

3 carrots, diced

2 celery sticks, diced

2 leeks, very thinly sliced

3 garlic cloves, chopped

1 dried red chilli

3 tomatoes, skinned, seeded and chopped

2 tablespoons tomato purée

4 leaves *cavolo nero* or outer leaves of savoy cabbage, tough stalks removed, leaves shredded

salt and freshly ground black pepper

TO SERVE:

6 slices stale bread

1 garlic clove, halved

best extra virgin olive oil

Make a bouquet garni by tying the rosemary, thyme and bay leaves together with a piece of string. Drain the beans, then place them in a large saucepan with about twice their volume of water and the bouquet garni. Don't add any salt or they will remain as tough as old boots. Bring up to the boil, boil hard for 10 minutes, then reduce the heat and simmer gently until very tender – 1½–2 hours depending on their age – adding more water if needed. When they are tender, draw off the heat and leave to cool in their cooking water.

Heat the oil in a large, heavy pot and add the onion, carrots, celery, leeks, chopped garlic and chilli. Cover and sweat over a low heat for about 10 minutes, stirring once or twice. Now uncover, add the tomatoes and tomato purée and cook for a further 3–4 minutes over a moderate heat. Then add the beans, their cooking water and enough water to cover all the vegetables. Season generously. Bring to the boil and simmer gently for half an hour, until the vegetables are all tender. Liquidize about half the contents of the pan, then return to the soup.

Add the shredded cabbage and simmer for a further 10 minutes, until tender. Taste and adjust the seasonings.

Meanwhile, rub the stale bread with the cut side of the halved garlic, and arrange in a warm, shallow dish or a wide tureen. When the soup is ready and really thick, spoon over the bread and serve immediately, putting a bottle of best olive oil out on the table for people to drizzle over their soup.

RIBOLLITA

BEAN AND VEGETABLE SOUP GRATIN

Ribollita means 'reboiled', and that is exactly what this 'soup' is. Actually, it is not really what we think of as a soup at all, since it becomes just about thick enough to eat with a fork. It is one of Tuscany's most famous dishes and, when it is made well, is wonderful, heart-warming comfort food.

It all begins with the *Zuppa di Verdura* on page 26. Originally, *ribollita* was a way to use up leftovers but it is so good that it is worth making the *zuppa* just to transform it into a *ribollita*. The reboiled soup is layered with stale bread and then baked in the oven until sizzling hot and savoury. A total triumph of thrift. I like the versions with slices of red onion baked on the surface, turning it sweet and juicy, a marvellous contrast to the thick, mealy *ribollita*. However, the slices of red onion are sometimes served on the side, sprinkled with salt, so that mouthfuls of fresh salted onion can be alternated with spoonfuls of the soup.

SERVES 6 AS A FIRST COURSE, 4 AS A MAIN COURSE

- **1 quantity *Zuppa di Verdura* (see page 26), made up to the point just before the *cavolo nero* is added**
- **6 slices good-quality, stale bread**
- **1 garlic clove, halved**
- **6 leaves *cavolo nero*, or outer leaves of savoy cabbage, thick stalks cut out, leaves coarsely chopped**
- **½–1 red onion, very finely sliced**
- **4 tablespoons freshly grated Parmesan cheese (optional)**
- **2–3 tablespoons extra virgin olive oil, plus extra for serving**

Once the soup is made, leave overnight. Next day, pre-heat the oven to 190°C/375°F/Gas Mark 5. Rub the stale bread with the cut side of the garlic. Bring the soup to the boil again and stir in the *cavolo nero* or cabbage. Oil a large gratin dish, or similar ovenproof dish, and spoon about a quarter of the soup into the dish, spreading it over the base. Now lay half the slices of bread over the soup, then spoon over half the remaining soup. Repeat these two layers one more time. Lay the sliced red onion over the top, then scatter with a little Parmesan, if you wish. Drizzle over a little olive oil and then bake for about 30 minutes.

Serve sizzling hot, with extra olive oil for those that want it.

SOCCA
ROASTED CHICKPEA PANCAKE

Socca is the street pancake of Nice, sold from great big metal dishes, hot and salty, with the golden tan of the chickpea flour that it is made with, browned and crisp at the edges, soft and tender inside. It reappears under a different name – *farinata* – not a million miles away, just across the Italian border in Liguria.

Inevitably, it tastes best eaten warm and crisp straight from the vendor out in the sun-strewn salty sea air. Nonetheless, it is worth tackling at home, because you can recapture most of its charm in your own kitchen. Serve it with drinks before supper, torn into rough squares, as a streetwise Mediterranean preamble to the main event, or use it in place of bread or potatoes. Cut into wedges, it can be dished up as part of a first course, plated up with a little rocket, a tumble of cherry tomatoes and mozzarella or feta, dressed with balsamic vinegar and extra virgin olive oil. Or take the street-market feel straight to the table – put the hot pan in the centre, let your guests tear off pieces as big or small as they like, and add a selection of small salads and cheeses for them to dig into as well.

Now, if you and your guests are sensible, self-moderating sorts, then this quantity will do for six of you served with drinks, or possibly as part of a first course. In my household, where self-moderation is a rare commodity, at least when it comes to great food, this would stretch around four at a pinch. If the dimensions of your roasting tin are a little larger than mine, increase the quantity of chickpea flour (which, incidentally, is sold in Indian food shops as gram flour) to 175 g (6 oz), and increase the water to a full 450 ml (15 fl oz).

SERVES 4–6

150 g (5 oz) chickpea flour
1 level teaspoon salt
375 ml (13 fl oz) water
3 tablespoons extra virgin olive oil, for the pan
½ level tablespoon finely chopped fresh rosemary (optional)
freshly ground black pepper

Sift the chickpea flour with the salt into a bowl. Make a well in the middle. Whisk in the water gradually to form a thin smooth batter. Leave to rest for 1–2 hours.

Pre-heat the oven to 220°C/425°F/Gas Mark 7. Spoon the oil into a 24 x 31 cm (9½ x 12½ inches) roasting tin and heat through in the oven for 3–4 minutes. Stir the chickpea batter once more and then pour into the hot tin, scatter over the rosemary, if using, and return immediately to the oven. Bake for 10–15 minutes, until the mixture is set and brown around the edges. Take out of the oven and season with black pepper. Let it stand for 5 minutes. Cut into squares or strips, or just tear up and serve.

TUSCAN CROSTINI
WITH CHICKEN LIVERS

This is the ubiquitous, incredibly good Tuscan *crostino* – they even sell the sauce ready-made in delicatessens. The bowls of pale brown sludge don't look too attractive but that doesn't put off anyone in the know. The sauce tastes superb (I rather like it on pasta, though it looks even less pretty that way), especially when freshly made, and you can always prettify the *crostini* once the sauce is smeared thickly over them with a few sprigs of herbal greenery (flatleaf parsley or a sprig of marjoram, perhaps) or with shavings of Parmesan and a light dusting of cayenne pepper.

SERVES 4

4 tablespoons extra virgin olive oil
45 g (1½ oz) unsalted butter
1 carrot, very finely chopped
1 celery stick, finely chopped
1 red onion, finely chopped
250 g (9 oz) chicken livers, cleaned and
  finely chopped
1 garlic clove, finely chopped
4 tablespoons semi-secco Marsala
3 tablespoons dry white wine
½ tablespoon tomato purée
1 tablespoon capers, thoroughly rinsed if salted
3 tinned anchovy fillets, roughly chopped
freshly ground black pepper

TO SERVE:

8 small slices bread (French baguette style, or
  halved slices of *pain de campagne*)
chopped fresh parsley
shavings of Parmesan cheese
cayenne pepper

Heat the oil with half the butter and add the carrot, celery and onion. Cook over a moderate heat, stirring frequently, for about 10 minutes until softened and lightly coloured. Add the chicken livers and garlic and cook for a few minutes more. Add the two wines and the tomato purée, raise the heat and boil hard until the wine has virtually evaporated, leaving just a thin film of liquid on the base. Cover and cook very gently for a further 10 minutes. Now stir in all the remaining ingredients and mix well. Then scrape into the processor and process briefly (or chop very finely) in short bursts, to give a coarse mix.

Toast or griddle the bread and spread with the chicken-liver mixture. Top with a little chopped parsley, a shaving of Parmesan and a very light dusting of cayenne pepper.

CROSTINI
WITH MOZZARELLA AND ANCHOVY

Fresh buffalo-milk mozzarella is nothing like the rubbery white cows'-milk version. Buffalo mozzarella is soft and tender and milky and here, as it melts in its stringy way, it softens the salty piquancy of the anchovies and sun-dried tomatoes.

4 slices good, sturdy bread

FOR THE TOPPING:
2 balls buffalo mozzarella, sliced
30 g (1 oz) unsalted butter
1 tablespoon extra virgin olive oil
8 pieces sun-dried tomatoes, cut roughly into strips
4 tinned anchovy fillets, drained and
  roughly chopped
2 garlic cloves, finely chopped
1–2 fresh rosemary sprigs
freshly ground black pepper
4 fresh mint sprigs, to garnish

Griddle or grill the bread. Lay slices of mozzarella on the toasted bread and place under the grill until melting.

Meanwhile, heat the butter with the olive oil and add the sun-dried tomatoes, anchovies, garlic and a sprig or two of rosemary. Sizzle gently, stirring, for about a minute. Discard the sprigs of rosemary, then pour the flavoured butter and bits over the hot *crostini*, season with pepper and top each with a sprig of mint.

ACEITUNAS GORDALES EN ALIÑO
SPANISH OLIVES, MARINATED WITH LEMON, GARLIC AND PEPPERS

As I whiled away the time between ordering and receiving my meal, the waiter placed a small plate of green olives marinated with a tumble of diced vegetables and citrus fruit before me on the table. The olives were massive – *gordales*, the fat ones, grown locally around Seville – and lightly scented. Soon, all that remained of them was a pile of stones.

When I got home, I was delighted to notice a stack of jars of Gordal olives on the shelves of my local supermarket. Hurray. I took them, I marinated them and, reader, do you know, they were very good, even without the Spanish sunshine. Of course, you can give any kind of green olive this treatment (but not black ones, which would be better off with just garlic, chilli, aromatic herbs and lashings of olive oil) as long as it has not been stoned and stuffed. Note, too, that this is just a short-term marinade and, although the mixture will keep for a few days in the fridge, it does not have long-term staying power. Freshness and vigour is the name of the olive game here.

SERVES 8–10
2 x 350 g (12 oz) jars Gordal green olives, or other
  green olives with stones in, drained
½ green pepper, seeded and diced
1 red pepper, seeded and diced
1 carrot, diced
½ lemon, diced (with the skin on)
½ orange, diced (with the skin on)
8 garlic cloves, not peeled, just bashed to half
  squash them
white wine vinegar

Mix all the solid ingredients. Pour over equal quantities of white wine vinegar and water, almost to cover the olives. Cover with cling film or a lid and leave to marinate for at least 8 hours. Drain before serving.

CHAPTER TWO

SALADS

MOROCCAN GREEN PEPPER AND PRESERVED LEMON SALAD

When I ate this salad in Morocco it was made of grilled green peppers and preserved lemon and nothing more, and it was marvellous. The trouble with such an elemental approach in this country is that our green peppers are different; when grilled, they develop a mildly bitter flavour which can be tremendous in combination with other ingredients but is too powerful to stand more or less on its own. Unless I can get hold of the long, tapering, narrow, sweet green peppers that taste more like Moroccan ones, I prefer to soften the strong taste of ordinary green peppers with the addition of diced tomato. This trio of green, yellow and red blends in great harmony, providing a deeply savoury contrast to some of the sweeter salads of the Moroccan table, though it is so good that it can stand as a side-dish on its own, served with fish, or a herb-strewn omelette.

SERVES 4

3 green peppers, grilled, skinned and seeded (see page 15)
3 ripe, well flavoured tomatoes (optional), seeded and finely diced
½ preserved lemon (see page 132), pulp discarded, skin finely diced
3 tablespoons chopped fresh flatleaf parsley
1 tablespoon lemon juice
1½ tablespoons extra virgin olive oil
salt and freshly ground black pepper

Mix all the ingredients, then taste and adjust the seasoning. Serve lightly chilled or at room temperature, having drained off excess dressing.

THE SEVERNSHED'S BAZARGAN

The Severnshed in Bristol is one of the new wave of restaurants taking inspiration from the cooking of the Middle East and North Africa. In fact they describe their food as 'modern Middle Eastern organic' and the results are quite wonderful. When my friend and producer, Mary Clyne, came back raving over this salad, I thought I'd better try it, so I begged for the recipe to try cooking it at home. Bazargan is a traditional Syrian dish, adopted by the Damascene Jewish community and generally associated with Friday dinners, but this version has been updated by Raviv Hadad, head chef at the Severnshed.

The surprising combination of cauliflower, cracked wheat, nuts, spices and pomegranate molasses is inspirational. Serve it as a starter, or even a vegetarian main course for a summer's day, with good bread. Pomegranate syrup is available from some good supermarkets, usually from their specialist shelves, and from Middle Eastern groceries. It has a fruity, tart flavour which is tremendous in salads.

SERVES 6–8

350 g (12 oz) bulgar (cracked wheat)
¼ cauliflower, broken into small florets
8 rosy red radishes, quartered
handful fresh flatleaf parsley, finely chopped
100 g (4 oz) hazelnuts, toasted and coarsely chopped
50 g (2 oz) pine nuts, toasted and coarsely chopped
150 g (5 oz) walnuts, toasted and coarsely chopped

FOR THE DRESSING:

½ teaspoon allspice berries
1 teaspoon coriander seeds
1 teaspoon cumin seeds
220 ml (8 fl oz) extra virgin olive oil
85 ml (3 fl oz) pomegranate syrup
150 ml (5 fl oz) tomato purée
juice and finely grated zest of 1 lemon
1 red chilli (or more), seeded and finely chopped
salt

Place the bulgar in a bowl, season with salt and cover with cold water. Leave to soak for about an hour, until *al dente*, that is, tender but still with a slight chewiness to it. Drain thoroughly, squeezing out excess water.

While the bulgar is soaking, dry-fry the spices briefly to crisp them, then let them cool. Pound to a powder in a mortar, or grind in an electric spice/coffee grinder.

To make the dressing, whisk the oil with the pomegranate syrup, tomato purée, lemon juice and zest, spices and chilli. The dressing will last for 3 or 4 days, in the fridge, covered, so it can be prepared well in advance.

Now mix the drained bulgar with cauliflower, radishes, parsley, nuts and the dressing. Spoon into a serving bowl, and place on the table.

CHAPTER THREE

VEGETABLE
DISHES

PUMPKIN AND FETA GRATIN

I shall have to come clean about this recipe – it isn't a traditional Mediterranean recipe at all, but one that is merely inspired by the spirit of warm country cooking. All around the Mediterranean, various forms of squash are used in cooking, often partnered with salty cheese which emphasizes the natural sweetness of the vegetable. Here I've linked it with both Greek feta and Italian Parmesan, in a gratin, which can be served as a side-dish or a light main course, hot or warm.

SERVES 4–8

2 kg (4½ lb) winter squash – pumpkin will do, but butternut, red kuri, crown
    prince or onion squash are much better
60 g (2 oz) butter
150 g (5 oz) feta cheese, drained and chopped or crumbled
85 g (3 oz) freshly grated Parmesan cheese
110 g (4 oz) breadcrumbs
3 tablespoons extra virgin olive oil
salt and freshly ground pepper

Halve the squash if it is a whole one, then remove the fibrous mass of seeds. Cut into long slices about 2.5–3.5 cm (1–1½ inches) thick. You can cut the skin from the slices now, or after the initial cooking, which I think is marginally easier and quicker. Bring a large pan of salted water to the boil, then add the squash slices (you may have to cook them in two batches). Bring back to the boil and then simmer for about 5–10 minutes, until the flesh is just tender (but not soggy). Drain thoroughly, then remove the skin, if you haven't already.

Pre-heat the oven to 200°C/400°F/Gas Mark 6. Use a generous knob of the butter to grease a shallow ovenproof dish (I use a 35 cm/14 inch gratin dish). Arrange the squash in it, scattering the crumbled feta over the squash as you go. Dot with the remaining butter, then season with salt and plenty of pepper. Mix the Parmesan with the breadcrumbs and scatter evenly over the squash. Drizzle the olive oil over the top. Bake for about 30 minutes, turning the dish around half-way through cooking if necessary, until evenly browned and crisp on top. Serve hot or warm.

CHAPTER FOUR

EGG & CHEESE DISHES

FRITTATA ALLA TRIPPA

PARMESAN AND PARSLEY OMELETTE
WITH FRESH TOMATO SAUCE

If ever there was a name of a dish designed to confuse, this has to be it. Literally translated it means 'tripe omelette', from which most of us would deduce that it meant an omelette made with tripe. But it doesn't. There isn't a single shred of anything remotely tripey in it at all. Purely vegetarian – a homely, but excellent dish from Siena, that we first encountered in a small restaurant, Il Caroccio, just off the miraculously beautiful Piazza del Campo. I'm glad to say that it wasn't just we pig-ignorant foreigners who misunderstood the name – so did our Sienese-born guide, but a look of recognition spread across her face when all was revealed; she knew the dish well, but wasn't so familiar with the name. It is, in fact, an omelette flavoured with Parmesan and parsley, and then cut up into strips, rather like tripe, and finished with a fresh tomato sauce – again, rather like tripe, in Italy at any rate.

Serve the tripe-style omelette as a light meal with bread and salads, or tucked into a warm roll with a smear of sauce, or as a first course.

SERVES 1 AS A MAIN COURSE, 2–3 AS
A FIRST COURSE (WITH SAUCE LEFT
OVER)

3 large eggs
15 g (½ oz) Parmesan cheese, freshly grated
1 tablespoon chopped fresh flatleaf parsley
salt and freshly ground black pepper
extra virgin olive oil, for frying

FOR THE SAUCE:

2 garlic cloves, chopped
2 tablespoons extra virgin olive oil
500 g (1 lb 2 oz) fresh tomatoes, skinned, seeded
** and chopped**
1 tablespoon tomato purée
salt and freshly ground black pepper
sugar

Whisk together the eggs, Parmesan, parsley, salt and pepper. Set aside.

To make the sauce, cook the garlic in the oil for a few seconds until just beginning to brown. Add the fresh tomatoes, tomato purée, salt, pepper and around 1 teaspoon of sugar. Cook hard for 3 minutes or so, until lightly thickened to form a lumpy, zippy tomato sauce. Taste and adjust the seasoning. Reheat briefly when needed.

Make the omelette shortly before serving. Heat the olive oil in a 28 cm (11 inch) frying-pan over a moderately high heat. Pour in the omelette mixture and swirl the pan to cover the base entirely. Reduce the heat and cook more gently until the surface is just set but not dry. Carefully loosen the edges from the side of the pan, then invert on to a plate. Put the pan back on to the heat, then slide the frittata back in, cooked-side up. Cook for a further minute or two just to set the underneath. Flip the sides over the middle and then turn out on to a warm serving plate. Quickly cut into ribbons about 1 cm (½ inch) wide. Spoon over about two-thirds of the sauce (save the rest to dress vegetables or a small portion of pasta) and serve immediately.

FRIED HALLÓUMI SALAD

Everyone knows the classic Greek salad, one of the best salads of the Mediterranean. Well, this is a variation on the theme, which, with its hot, salty, fried cheese, becomes a light main course in itself. The majority of the salad ingredients can be assembled (but not tossed into the dressing) an hour or two ahead of time, and then covered and stored in the fridge until quarter of an hour before serving, but don't fry the cheese until the very last minute.

Just in case you need a reminder, a straight Greek salad is made with chunks of juicy, ripe tomato, thick, peeled cucumber crescents, thinly sliced rings of onion, sometimes with the addition of shredded cos lettuce, and rings of green pepper. On top sits a fine slab of feta cheese, sprinkled with dried oregano. The whole salad is dotted with crinkly black olives, and dressed with good olive oil, wine vinegar or lemon juice, salt and pepper.

Place the cos lettuce in a wide, shallow bowl and arrange the tomatoes, olives, cucumber, quails' eggs (if using) and skinned peppers over it. Cover with cling film and keep cool for up to 2 hours. Bring back to room temperature before finishing the salad.

To make the dressing, whisk the oil with the lemon juice, *rígani* or oregano, salt and pepper. Set aside until needed.

Shortly before serving, heat the 2 tablespoons of oil over a high heat. Fry the hallóumi or kephalotiri briskly until browned on all sides. As soon as it is done, lay the cheese on the salad. Quickly whisk the dressing one last time and then spoon over the cheese and the salad. Toss at the table and serve quickly, while the hallóumi or kephalotiri is still warm.

SERVES 4–6

1 cos lettuce, thickly shredded

170 g (6 oz) cherry tomatoes, halved

12–18 kalamata olives

1 cucumber, peeled, halved lengthways and cut in thick half moons

8 quails' eggs, boiled, shelled and halved (optional)

1 red pepper, grilled, skinned, seeded and cut into strips

1 green pepper, grilled, skinned, seeded and cut into strips

2 tablespoons extra virgin olive oil

250 g (9 oz) hallóumi or kephalotiri cheese, drained and cut into 1 cm (½ inch) wide batons

FOR THE DRESSING:

3 tablespoons extra virgin olive oil

juice of ½ large lemon

2 teaspoons *rígani* or dried oregano

salt and freshly ground black pepper

CHAK-CHOUKA

BAKED EGGS IN SPICED PEPPER AND TOMATO STEW

This mixture of fried peppers, tomatoes, and eggs, flavoured with cumin, comes from the southern part of the Mediterranean, from Tunisia and its neighbouring countries, where it might be served for breakfast. Back at home you may well prefer to serve it as a starter, or as a light main course for lunch or supper.

SERVES 6 AS A STARTER, 2–3 AS A MAIN COURSE

5 tablespoons extra virgin olive oil

2 onions, sliced

2 garlic cloves, sliced

1 small green pepper, seeded and cut into long, thin strips

1 small red pepper, seeded and cut into long, thin strips

1 heaped teaspoon ground cumin, plus a little extra for serving

500 g (1 lb 2 oz) ripest tomatoes, skinned, and roughly chopped

1 tablespoon tomato purée

1 teaspoon caster sugar, if needed

6 eggs

cayenne pepper or paprika

salt and freshly ground black pepper

Heat the oil in a heavy-based frying-pan, over a moderate heat. Add the onions, garlic and peppers and fry, stirring frequently, until soft and floppy (this will take some 10–15 minutes, so don't try to hurry it). Stir in the cumin, and fry for another minute. Next, add the tomatoes, with any juice that has oozed out of them, the tomato purée, salt and pepper, and a touch of sugar if the tomatoes are very sharp. Allow the mixture to cook to a thick, but wettish, sauce. Taste and adjust the seasoning.

Make a dip in the vegetable mixture with the back of a spoon, then break an egg into it. Repeat with the remaining eggs. When all the eggs are in, cover the frying-pan with a lid or large plate and continue cooking gently for a further 8–10 minutes, until the eggs are set. Sprinkle the eggs with a little more salt and a light dusting of cumin and cayenne pepper or paprika and serve.

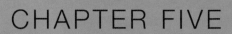

CHAPTER FIVE

PIZZA, PASTA & RICE

ROCKET PIZZA

There's been quite a revolution going in the pizza parlour over the past few years. For inspiration, *pizzaiolo* (pizza makers) are turning back to their roots, to Italy, often combining the old classic thin-crust pizzas with thoroughly contemporary ideas. One of the best is the rocket pizza. The combination of fresh, peppery greenery, tomato, cheese and crisp pizza base is terrific. Taleggio cheese adds spots of decadent creamy richness but, if you can't get it, don't panic – these pizzas will still taste fantastic.

MAKES 2 PIZZAS

FOR THE DOUGH:

400 g (14 oz) strong white bread flour
2 level teaspoons salt
½ teaspoon caster sugar
1 sachet easy-blend yeast
2 tablespoons extra virgin olive oil

FOR THE TOMATO SAUCE:

1 x 400 g (14 oz) tin chopped tomatoes in tomato juice
2 garlic cloves, crushed
1 tablespoon extra virgin olive oil
1 bay leaf
2 fresh parsley sprigs
1 fresh thyme sprig
salt and freshly ground black pepper

FOR THE TOPPING:

1 tablespoon capers, rinsed and soaked if salted
6 pieces sun-dried tomato, roughly shredded
1 ball buffalo-milk mozzarella, sliced
150 g (5 oz) taleggio cheese, rinded and cubed as best you can (optional)
extra virgin olive oil
75–100 g (3–4 oz) fresh rocket
salt and freshly ground black pepper

To make the dough, mix the flour with the salt, sugar and yeast and make a well in the centre. Add the olive oil and enough water to mix to a soft, slightly sticky dough. Flour your hands and then gather your dough up into a ball. Knead vigorously on a lightly floured work surface for a good 8–10 minutes, until satiny smooth and elastic. Rinse the bowl out, dry, and dust with flour. Place the dough in the bowl, turn to coat lightly in the flour and then cover with a damp cloth and leave in a warm place for about an hour, until doubled in size.

Meanwhile, make the sauce. Put all the ingredients into a saucepan and simmer for about 20 minutes until thick, stirring occasionally. Taste and adjust the seasoning, then remove the herbs and cool.

Put two baking sheets in the oven and pre-heat to 230°C/450°F/Gas Mark 8. Punch down the dough. Gather together and knead again for a few minutes. Divide in two. Using your hands and a rolling pin, stretch the first ball of dough out to form a circle 25 cm (10 inches) across. When it is about right, use your fingers to push dough to the edges, forming a thick rim. Lay on another well floured flat baking sheet (or a board, or even a piece of stiff cardboard, as long as it is well floured). Smear half the tomato sauce over the pizza, leaving the rim bare. Dot with half the capers, sun-dried tomato, mozzarella and taleggio. Drizzle a thin trickle of olive oil over the top. Make a second pizza in the same way.

Open the oven and carefully shake and slide the pizzas on to the hot baking sheets inside. Bake for 15–20 minutes until the edges are browned and the cheese is sizzling.

Just before serving, divide the rocket between the two pizzas, piling it casually over the surface. Drizzle over a last shot of olive oil, grind a little pepper over the top, and serve, with the rocket just beginning to soften here and there in the heat of the pizzas.

FUSILLI AL ZUCOTTO CON ROSMARINO

PASTA WITH PUMPKIN AND ROSEMARY

Badia a Coltibuono is set high up in the Tuscan hills, north-west of Siena. From this beautiful place come some of the finest of Tuscan olive oils. You can buy the oils directly from the shop here, as well as vinegars, fabulous honey (my favourite is the chestnut flower honey with an almost burnt edge to its sweetness) and other culinary gems. The neat, modern restaurant, tucked away in the woods beside the church, serves superb local food, which is perhaps not surprising as the whole enterprise is run by food-writer Lorenza di Medici and her daughter and fellow food-writer, Emmanuella. When we ate there one gloriously sunny, early autumn day, they gave us an excellent dish of pasta dressed with buttery pumpkin and rosemary. This is my version of their original.

SERVES 4 AS A STARTER, 2–3 AS A MAIN COURSE
400 g (14 oz) fusilli
4 small fresh rosemary sprigs, to garnish (optional)
freshly grated Parmesan cheese, to serve

FOR THE SAUCE:
85 g (3 oz) unsalted butter
1 garlic clove, crushed
450 g (1 lb) peeled and seeded pumpkin or butternut squash, cut into 1 cm
  (½ inch) dice
1 teaspoon very finely chopped fresh rosemary
finely grated zest of ½ lemon
freshly grated nutmeg
salt and pepper

Put a large pan of well salted water on to boil. When it is at a rolling boil, tip in the fusilli and cook until *al dente*. Drain.

Meanwhile, melt the butter in a wide saucepan. Add the garlic and stir about for 30 seconds or so, then add the pumpkin, rosemary, lemon zest, salt, pepper and nutmeg. Cover and sweat over a gentle heat for about 15 minutes, stirring occasionally, until the pumpkin is very soft. Squash a little of it down into the butter but leave about two-thirds more or less as it is. Taste and adjust the seasoning. Re-heat if necessary, when the pasta is cooked.

Return the drained pasta to the pan, add the pumpkin sauce and mix lightly. Serve immediately, tucking a decorative sprig of rosemary, if using, into each helping. Pass the Parmesan and enjoy.

CHAPTER SIX

FISH & SHELLFISH

BAKED HALIBUT WITH TOMATO AND OREGANO

The firm, milky white flesh of halibut makes it ideal for baking in steaks, under a layer of tomatoes and breadcrumbs, which doubles as both crisp topping and sauce. I like to keep this simple but you could add chopped olives or capers or both, for a piquant touch, or perhaps replace the oregano with a tablespoon or more of chopped fennel leaf.

SERVES 4

**675 g (1½ lb) halibut (or cod) steaks, cut about
2.5 cm (1 inch) thick**
5 tablespoons extra virgin olive oil
**500 g (1 lb 2 oz) tomatoes, skinned, seeded and
finely chopped**
2 garlic cloves, finely chopped
1 tablespoon dried oregano, crumbled
2 tablespoons chopped fresh parsley
1 teaspoon caster sugar
4 tablespoons soft breadcrumbs
salt and freshly ground black pepper

Pre-heat the oven to 200°C/400°F/Gas Mark 6. Season the halibut with salt and freshly ground black pepper. Use a little of the oil to oil an ovenproof dish, just large enough to take the halibut steaks in a snug single layer. Lay the halibut in it. Mix 3½ tablespoons of the olive oil with the tomatoes, garlic, oregano, parsley, sugar, salt and pepper. Spoon over the fish, then scatter breadcrumbs evenly over the top. Drizzle over the remaining olive oil. Bake for about 20–25 minutes, until the crumbs are crisp and the fish is just cooked through.

BARBECUED GARLIC KING PRAWNS

WITH BOILED-LEMON, AVOCADO AND TOMATO SALAD

A few years ago, I watched Ruth Rogers and Rose Gray of the River Café make a boiled-lemon salad. It made a big impact on me - what an extraordinary idea, but why not? Finally, my curiosity came to fruition; I tried boiling lemons in the comfort of my own home, just to find out what they were like. The result is very tender-fleshed morsels that pack in all kinds of flavours – tart, bitter and aromatic all at once. Too strong to be eaten neat, I felt, they nonetheless make a brilliant addition to salads, and are just perfect with the smooth, buttery texture of avocados. The addition of sizzling, garlicky prawns turns the avocado, lemon and tomato salad into a fresh and vibrant starter or main course for a light summer meal al fresco.

SERVES 4

12–16 raw tiger or king prawns, shell on
4 garlic cloves, very finely chopped
1 red chilli, seeded and finely chopped
1 tablespoon lemon juice
4 tablespoons extra virgin olive oil
salt and freshly ground black pepper

FOR THE SALAD:

1 lemon
1 avocado
110 g (4 oz) cherry tomatoes, halved, or 2 medium-
**   sized ripe, sweet tomatoes, sliced**
3 tablespoons chopped fresh coriander

FOR THE DRESSING:

4 tablespoons extra virgin olive oil
2 tablespoons lemon juice
salt and freshly ground black pepper

Bring a pan of salted water to the boil. Prick the lemon in three or four places and then place in the boiling water. Boil for about 50 minutes, until very tender. Drain and leave to cool. Slice off the ends and discard. Dice the rest, skin, flesh and all.

Place the prawns in a shallow dish or bowl. Mix together the garlic, chilli, lemon juice, olive oil, salt and pepper and pour over. Cover and leave to marinate for at least an hour in the fridge; 3–4 hours will be even more effective.

To make the dressing for the salad, whisk the olive oil with the lemon juice and season with salt and pepper. Taste and adjust the seasoning, keeping the dressing on the tart side.

Pre-heat the barbecue (or grill) thoroughly. Shortly before serving, halve, skin and slice the avocado, and toss in a spoonful or two of the dressing. Pick the prawns out of the marinade and then put them on to grill – give them about 2–3 minutes on each side, basting with the marinade after turning, until they become rosy pink.

Quickly assemble the salad – mix the avocado with the tomatoes, boiled lemon and coriander. Either place in a bowl, and serve the prawns on a separate serving dish, or make a mound of salad on each individual plate and arrange 3–4 prawns around it. Serve at once.

SEARED O
TUNA STE/
WITH TAPENADE

Fresh tuna is an end
sturdy enough to ma
pungent flavours of F
(garlic mayonnaise) a
with great aplomb. T
of the serving plate c
rocket, partially cook
flavour a little.

SERVES 4
4 x tuna steaks, weig
  (6–8 oz) each
juice of 1 lemon
extra virgin olive oil
2 handfuls of rocket
4 tablespoons *Tapen;*
6–8 tablespoons *Aïoli*
salt and freshly groun

About half an hour be
steaks with half the le
massaging it gently ir

Whisk the rest of the
tablespoons of extra
and reserve.

To cook, wipe the fish
sear or grill or barbecu
Grilled Tuna with Cher
cooks, quickly toss the
dressing. Either spread
make four beds of roc
plates. Place a spoonf
aïoli beside the rocket,
otherwise, just place tl
arrange on the table. /
lay it on top of the dres
wilt in the heat of the t
fish's juice. Serve swift

SEARED OR GRILLED TUNA WITH CHERMOULA

Chermoula (or *charmoula*) is a nigh-on-miraculous blend of herbs, spices and lemon juice that Moroccans love to use with fish. I like it best with stronger-tasting fish, like meaty tuna, or sardines. While *chermoula*-coated tuna is perfect for the barbecue or for searing in a hot pan, sardines demand a slightly different treatment – beheaded and boned (a kind fishmonger will do this for you), the fillets are sandwiched together with the *chermoula*, dipped into flour, then fried quickly in a finger-knuckle's depth of oil. Serve them just as they are or slip into warmed pitta pockets with diced tomato and cucumber.

Enough of sardines, this recipe puts the focus on tuna, which is an absolute natural with *chermoula*. Serve the quickly seared tuna (2 minutes a side cooks the flesh medium rare, leaving it moist and juicy) with a few new potatoes and a tomato or cos salad and you have a perfect summer lunch or supper dish.

SERVES 4
4 x tuna steaks, weighing about 175–225 g (6–8 oz) each
extra virgin olive oil

FOR THE *CHERMOULA*:
1 bunch fresh coriander (or ½ bunch coriander and ½ bunch fresh parsley)
2 teaspoons whole cumin seeds, toasted and crushed
½–1 teaspoon cayenne pepper
2 teaspoons sweet paprika
4 garlic cloves
juice of 1 lemon
2 tablespoons extra virgin olive oil
½ tablespoon coarse sea salt

To make the *chermoula*, put all the ingredients in the processor and process to a slightly uneven purée. Smear over the steaks on both sides. Place in a shallow dish, cover and leave to marinate for at least 2 hours, turning occasionally, before cooking.

To sear the fish, wipe a heavy frying-pan with olive oil. Place over a high heat and leave to heat through thoroughly for about 3 minutes. Lay the tuna in the pan and cook the steaks for about 2 minutes on each side. Serve immediately.

To grill, pre-heat the grill (or barbecue) thoroughly. Grill the tuna close to the heat for about 2 minutes on each side. Serve immediately.

GRIDDLED (OR BARBECUED) SQUID
WITH BASIL AND TOMATO SAUCE

Squid is one of the easiest of seafoods to cook, needing only a minute or so each side to firm it up to a particular sweet, firm succulence. Here, the griddled or barbecued squid is simply tarted up with a warm sauce of olive oil, basil and tomato when it comes sizzling hot to the plate.

When buying squid, look for whole fish (preferably that have not been previously frozen, though these are getting harder and harder to find, sadly) and, if you can't face preparing them yourself, ask the fishmonger to do it for you – but don't let him throw the tentacles out: they're the best bit.

If you don't fancy squid, you could use this sauce on all manner of seafood, from seabass or scallops through to grilled plaice or sardines.

SERVES 4

900 g–1 kg (2–2¼ lb) medium-sized squid, cleaned (see below)
1 tablespoon extra virgin olive oil
4 fresh basil sprigs, to serve
salt and freshly ground black pepper

FOR THE SAUCE:

150 ml (5 fl oz) extra virgin olive oil
2 fresh thyme sprigs
1 bay leaf
1 teaspoon coriander seeds, lightly crushed
2 ripe tomatoes, skinned, seeded and finely diced
½ tablespoon balsamic vinegar
handful fresh basil leaves, shredded
1 garlic clove, halved
coarse sea salt and freshly ground black pepper

Although the sauce is absolutely lovely made up just before using, it is even better if you make it a day or two in advance, so that the flavours have time to mingle and develop. It won't take long, because all you have to do is mix everything together. If you are keeping the sauce, cover with cling film and store in a cool place. The fridge is a bit cold but, if the weather's hot and there's no alternative, it will do.

To clean the squid, first grasp the head firmly with one hand and pull gently away from the body, bringing, with luck, all, but probably just some, of the innards with it. Fish about inside the body sac and pull out the clear, plastic-like 'quill' inside, as well as remaining gunk. Pull the mottled greyish purple skin off the outside of the body sac. Chop the tentacles off the head just above the eyes. Save body and tentacles and discard all the rest, unless you want to use the black ink for something (you could try making black pasta, or use it to flavour and colour a sauce, or just use it as fishy ink!). The ink sac is a small, long thin silvery bag tucked amongst the innards of the squid. It often gets punctured as the squid is handled, so if there are traces of black ink all around and no sign of it, then don't bother searching too hard – it is fairly easy to spot. When you do find it, cut it carefully away and drop it into a glass. To release the ink just stir vigorously with a metal spoon.

Pre-heat the barbecue thoroughly, if using. Slit open the squid bodies, rinse and pat dry. Make crisscross slashes on each piece of squid. If barbecuing, thread the tentacles loosely on to a skewer. If griddling, oil the griddle pan lightly, then place over a high heat for about 3-5 minutes to heat through. Meanwhile, pour the sauce into a saucepan and warm gently, without letting it boil. Keep warm. Brush the squid bodies on one side with oil and lay them, oil-side down, on the griddle. Don't worry too much about oiling the tentacles, just lay them straight on the griddle. Turn each piece of squid after about ¾–1 minute, and cook for the same amount of time on the other side.

Place on a serving dish, season with salt and pepper and spoon the sauce over. Serve at once with the fresh basil.

SPIEDINI DI CODA DI ROSPA ALLA SALVIA
MONKFISH AND PANCETTA KEBABS WITH SAGE

Monkfish is the best of all white fish to thread onto a skewer, because it holds together so well. Just to make doubly sure that it doesn't collapse, a band of pancetta is wrapped around each chunk of fish, to turn crisp in the heat of the barbecue or grill. The particular flavourings come in two forms: first as *salmoriglio*, a marinade straight from Sicily, and secondly as sage leaves that separate and scent the cubes of fish.

These kebabs are best cooked on a fearsomely hot barbecue but, failing that, make sure that you pre-heat your grill very, very thoroughly, and get the pancetta-wrapped fish as close as you reasonably can to the heat, so that it browns before it overcooks.

SERVES 4
700 g (1½ lb) monkfish fillet, cut into 4 cm (1½ inch) cubes, more or less
150 g (5 oz) pancetta
around 24 fresh sage leaves
salt and freshly ground black pepper

FOR THE SALMORIGLIO:
juice of 1½ lemons
8 tablespoons extra virgin olive oil
1 tablespoon dried oregano
2 garlic cloves, crushed
salt and freshly ground black pepper

Whisk together the *salmoriglio* ingredients and spoon half of it over the monkfish. Turn to coat thoroughly, then leave to marinate for at least half an hour.

Cut the strips of pancetta in half, as long as that leaves them long enough to wrap round each cube of monkfish. Now, take the monkfish out of the marinade and, one by one, wrap each cube in a length of pancetta. Slip it on to a skewer, so that the pancetta is held in place, alternating with sage leaves.

Cook over a thoroughly pre-heated barbecue (or under a thoroughly pre-heated grill), close to the heat, turning frequently, for about 8–10 minutes, until the pancetta is crisp and the monkfish just cooked through. Brush the kebabs with leftover marinade every now and then as they cook, and serve with the remaining half of the *salmoriglio*.

INSALATA DI MARE
SEAFOOD SALAD

This Italian seafood salad is one of the great joys of summer eating by the Italian seashore. Just the thought of it takes me straight to some idyllic restaurant terrace, perched high above the sparkling blue sea, with a gentle sea breeze softening the intense heat of midday, starched white table cloths, pearls of icy condensation on the bottle of crisp, white wine, the insistent trill of cicadas and the distant plash of waves echoing up the cliff... Forgive me while I dream.

It's not the quickest of dishes to make, but it is remarkably easy, as long as you buy the best and freshest shellfish and fish. You may need to order clams in advance from your fishmonger. There seems to me to be little point in making it in small quantity but, rest assured , if you only need half for a special starter for a lunch, the rest will keep well in the fridge for 24 hours, as long as you don't leave it lingering in a warm kitchen or dining room.

SERVES 8–10 AS A STARTER, 6–8 AS A LIGHT LUNCH DISH

3 strips of lemon zest

1 kg (generous 2 lb) palourdes or other small clams

1 kg (generous 2 lb) mussels, scrubbed clean, de-bearded and rinsed thoroughly

550 g (1¼ lb) squid, cleaned (see page 120)

500 g (1 lb) raw large prawns

1 medium sole (lemon or Dover), filleted and cut into 2 cm (¾ inch) wide strips

1 bunch fresh flat-leaved parsley, chopped

juice of 2 lemons

150 ml (5 fl oz) extra virgin olive oil

1 garlic clove, finely chopped

125 g (4½ oz) mixed baby salad leaves

175 g (6 oz) small cherry tomatoes, halved

6 fresh basil leaves, shredded

salt and freshly ground black pepper

Pour enough water into a large saucepan to cover the base by about 5 mm (¼ inch). Add the lemon zest to the pan and set over a high heat. Add the clams, cover tightly and shake over a high heat until the shells have opened – about 6 minutes, give or take. Scoop out the clams with a slotted spoon and transfer to a bowl. Discard any that refuse to open. Repeat the process with the mussels, heating them for about 5 minutes. Then scoop them into the bowl with the clams, again discarding any that refuse to open. Let the liquid in the saucepan settle, then strain through a fine sieve and return to the pan. Pick the mussel and clam meat out of the shells. Strain the juices left in the bowl into the cooking juices in the saucepan.

Clean the squid (see page 120) and cut the body into rings about 1 cm (½ inch) wide. Leave the tentacles clumped together in bunches. Bring the saucepan of juice back to the boil and add the squid. Simmer for about 1–2 minutes, until just white and opaque.Lift out with a slotted spoon and add to the mussels and clams. Drop the prawns into the juices (if they've boiled off too much, add a splash of hot water) and simmer for about 3 minutes, until they are pink and opaque. Scoop them out and allow to cool. Next, lay the strips of sole in the last of the simmering juice and cook for 30–60 seconds, until just opaque. Carefully lift them out and allow to cool. Peel the prawns, and de-vein them. Mix all the seafood, bar the sole, with the parsley, the juice of 1½ lemons, 8 tablespoons of olive oil, garlic, salt and pepper. Very carefully stir in the sole, trying not to break it up too much. Chill lightly in the fridge.

Whisk the remaining lemon juice with the remaining olive oil, 2 tablespoons of the cooking liquid, salt and pepper. Toss the baby lettuce in two-thirds of the dressing, and the halved tomatoes and basil in the remainder. Make a bed of lettuce on each plate. Mound the seafood salad on top. Arrange the tomatoes and basil around the edge and serve.

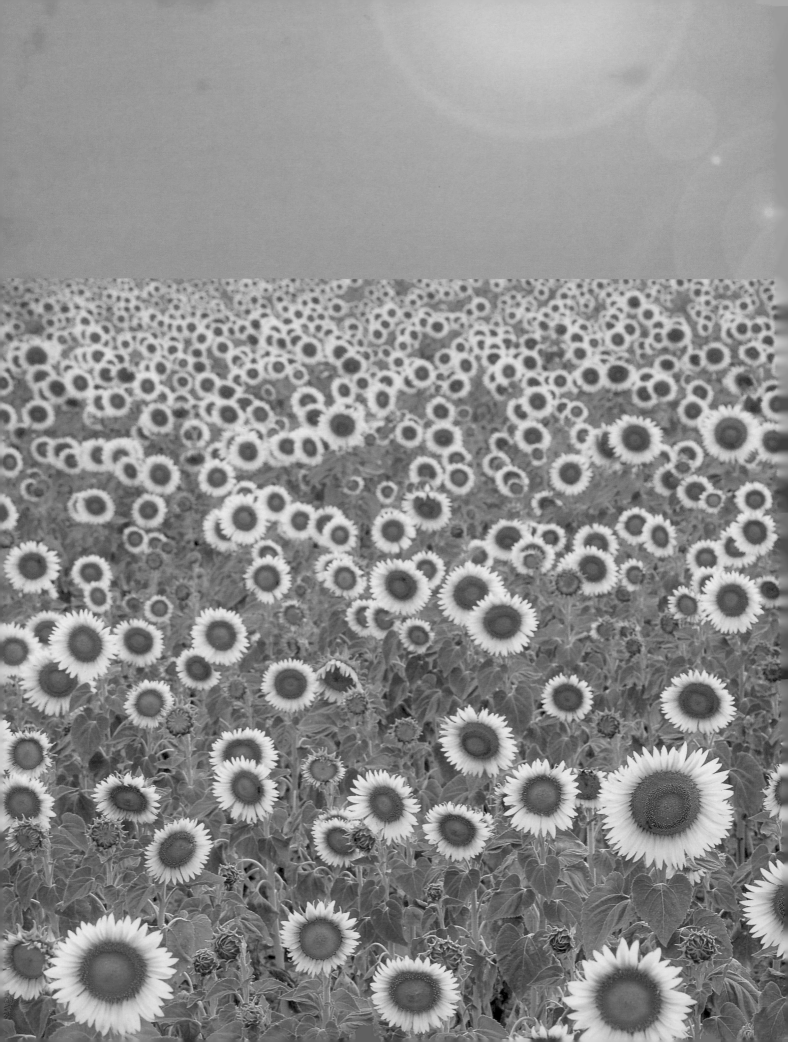

CHAPTER SEVEN

SAUCES & FLAVOURINGS

SALSA CRUDA
UNCOOKED TOMATO SAUCE

Though I've included the recipe for *salsa cruda* in other books, I can't resist putting it in again here. Made with first-rate tomatoes, sweet, juicy, aromatic and tart all rolled into one imperfect sphere, it becomes one of the essential Mediterranean sauces for clement weather – and perhaps even more essential on rainy-grey summer days, when you are desperate for something to remind you of the warmth of the sun.

The name means nothing more fancy than 'raw sauce', which is exactly what it is: tomatoes, shallots or onions, garlic, and basil, mixed together with a touch of lemon or vinegar and some olive oil. I love it cool and slightly chilled from the fridge, tossed into hot spaghetti, which releases a burst of flavour from the tomatoes and basil. That is only the most obvious of its uses. Like the very similar new world salsas, it can be used as a sauce-cum-relish with grilled meats and fish, or with deep-fried fritters. Give it a whirl, too, tossed with lentils or pasta, to make a cool salad – you'll probably need to increase the quantities of lemon juice and olive oil to bring the mealy texture of lentils or pasta into orbit.

If I fancy the panacea of this sauce when the season for summer tomatoes is past, I turn to little, sweet, juicy cherry tomatoes, which I quarter (without skinning – life is far too short for that) to make a chunkier version.

SERVES 4–6

500 g (1 lb 2 oz) fabulous tomatoes, skinned, seeded and finely chopped, or cherry tomatoes, quartered
½ small red or white onion, or 2 small shallots, very finely chopped
2 tablespoons extra virgin olive oil
1 tablespoon lemon juice or balsamic or sherry vinegar
1 garlic clove, very finely chopped
8 fresh basil leaves, torn up
salt and freshly ground black pepper
sugar, if needed

Mix all the ingredients, adding a pinch or two of sugar if you think the tomatoes need pepping up. Cover and chill for 20 minutes. Stir again, and taste, adding more olive oil, lemon juice, salt, pepper or sugar if needed.

SALSA VERDE
PIQUANT HERB SAUCE

This Italian green sauce is up there amongst my very favourite Mediterranean recipes. It has such a vibrant, energizing flavour, capturing all that is best about the food of the region – great generous handfuls of herbs, olives, capers, anchovies, garlic and fruity olive oil, blended together to a blessed unguent that brings life and delight to so many different dishes. Traditionally it is served with *Bollito Misto* (page 146) and other boiled meat dishes, but its role does not stop there. It is sensational with grilled or barbecued seafood (try it with monkfish or tuna, in particular), divine with roast or boiled vegetables, thrilling with roast, grilled, fried or poached poultry and so on, and so on.

There are, inevitably, a thousand and one or more versions, which is really part of the beauty of the sauce. Everyone who makes it can customize it for themselves – the size of the bunch of parsley is whatever you make it as long as you are generous, and take the opportunity to vary the balance of those piquant, salty ingredients until you find the right balance for your palate. If you don't like olives, leave them out and add a few more capers and an extra slug of vinegar. Try it, perhaps, with lemon juice instead of vinegar. Some versions include a few cornichons (mildly pickled baby gherkins), whilst others add the yolk of a hard-boiled egg, or a little mustard, or omit the mint or basil. If you have the time and inclination, chop the ingredients together by hand to achieve a coarser texture.

Anyway, once made with whatever variations you fancy, the sauce can be stored in the fridge (see the recipe) for several days, though it is at its best fresh from the processor.

SERVES 8–10

1 bunch fresh parsley
handful fresh basil leaves
handful fresh mint leaves
4 tinned anchovy fillets
2 tablespoons capers, rinsed, or thoroughly soaked
** if salted**
2 garlic cloves, roughly chopped
45 g (1½ oz) stoned green olives, roughly chopped
1–2 tablespoons red or white wine vinegar
1 tablespoon sugar
1 slice good-quality white bread, crusts removed,
** torn into pieces (about 50 g/2 oz)**
150–250 ml (5–9 fl oz) extra virgin olive oil
salt and freshly ground black pepper

Slash the leaves from the bunch of parsley and drop them into the processor. Add the basil and mint leaves and all the other ingredients, except the oil and salt. Process in short bursts, scraping down the sides in between bursts, until finely chopped. Keep the motor running and trickle in enough olive oil to make a thickish sauce. Taste and adjust the seasoning, adding more vinegar and salt only if needed. Pour into a bowl and serve.

If not using immediately, drizzle a little extra olive oil over the surface, then cover with cling film and store in the fridge until needed. Serve at room temperature, having stirred the extra oil into the sauce.

PRESERVED LEMONS

For me, the most exciting taste in all of Moroccan cooking is that of salt-preserved lemons. There is nothing else quite like it, and certainly no adequate substitutes. It is hard to describe, this full, soul-satisfying, electric yet soft flavour. It comes clearly from a lemon, no doubting that, since it has remnants of both the flavours of the zest and the juice, but the transformation that has taken place is remarkable. Probably the most renowned dish containing preserved lemons is *Djej Makali* (*Tagine of Chicken, Preserved Lemons and Olives*, page 164); but they also go marvellously with fish, and one of the nicest salads I ate on my last trip there was made of grilled green peppers and tiny squares of preserved lemon (*Moroccan Green Pepper and Preserved Lemon Salad*, page 44). Back at home, my husband came up with a particularly good salsa made of diced tomatoes, diced preserved lemon, finely chopped shallot and coriander, which goes very well with barbecued or grilled chicken, as well as grilled or griddled tuna, swordfish, or mackerel.

In Moroccan markets you can choose between tiny preserved lemons, about as big as a ping–pong ball, and big, golden, gleaming lemons, with protruding navels but, if you make them yourself here – and it is very easy to do – settle for the best looking, least blemished lemons that you can find. You can add extra seasonings, bay leaves, coriander seeds, cloves of garlic and the like but, to be frank, I think they are unnecessary, even if they do look pretty.

One word of warning – don't even think of attempting this recipe if you have any cuts or grazes on your hands. The pain of lemon juice and salt combined is excruciating.

FILLS A 1 LITRE (1 ¾ PINT)
PRESERVING JAR
8 unwaxed lemons
50–75 g (2–3 oz) coarse salt
2 bay leaves (optional)

Sterilize a 1 litre (1¾ pint) preserving jar (see page 19) and allow to cool, covered with a clean tea towel. When you are ready to go, sprinkle a heaped tablespoonful of the salt over the base.

Take a lemon and, with a sharp knife, make two cuts at right angles, starting from the stem end and finishing about 1 cm (½ inch) short of the other end, so that the lemon is cut almost into quarters, but still holds together. Open the fruit out a little and sprinkle the insides with a generous helping of salt, then reshape the lemon. Pack it down firmly in the preserving jar. Sprinkle with salt.

Repeat with another four lemons, pressing each one down firmly, so that they all squish into the jar, releasing some of their juice under the pressure of your hand.

Now add the juice of the remaining 3 lemons, and enough water to cover the semi–quartered and salted lemons completely. If you wish, you can tuck a couple of bay leaves down the sides of the jar. Now, cut two lengths of wooden skewer just a touch longer than the diameter of the opening of the jar. Using patience, a little brute force (but not too much or you will snap the wood), push them down under the rim of the jar, at right angles to each other, so that they force the lemons to remain submerged in the lemon juice and water. Seal the jar tightly and leave on a shelf, out of harm's reach, for about 4 weeks, before using.

When you need a lemon for a recipe, remove it from the lemon brine with a wooden spoon (not a metal one, which could discolour and taint the remaining lemons). Separate the quarters, cut away the inner pulp and discard. Cut the peel into strips, or as described in the recipe. The tart brine is useful too – excellent in salad dressings or in marinades, particularly for fish.

TAPENADE

Dark, pungent tapenade is one of the defining flourishes of Provençal food. A blend of black olives, capers (*tapena* is the Provençal word for capers), anchovies and a variable collection of other background elements, including, sometimes, tuna fish, it turns up here, there and everywhere – except in sweet dishes, naturally.

Although it can be made in smaller quantities, there seems little point in making less than this, since it keeps well in the fridge and can be used in so many ways. As a little *amuse-bouche* with an apéritif, spread tapenade thinly on griddled or baked croûtons of bread, or mash the yolks of halved hard-boiled eggs with a little mayonnaise or crème fraîche and tapenade to taste, then pile back into the whites to serve as an hors d'oeuvre (both tapenade croûtons and eggs are gorgeous with the *Peperonata* on page 56, both for the contrast of sweet and pungent flavours, crisp, soft and slippery textures and for the colours). Or make life easy for yourself and put the eggs (possibly even little boiled quails' eggs), tapenade, *Peperonata* and bread in bowls and plates on the table and let everyone help themselves. I love tapenade with tomatoes, particularly cherry tomatoes – stir a spoonful or two into the dressing for a salad, or just place it alongside. Moving on to the main course, smear it over or inside lamb, chicken or fish before roasting or, if you prefer, use it as a sauce to accompany the meat and small boiled or roast new potatoes.

The making of tapenade is easy; what is more testing is choosing the right olives. Chew on one before you buy, to make quite certain that you really like its taste. Don't buy them in a jar or tin, unless you know that you like the taste of that brand, and, above all, don't buy tinned stoned black olives, which, more often than not, taste soapy – something which will be sorrowfully emphasized in the tapenade. When the perfect small Niçoise olive is not on the cards, I find that the big juicy Greek Kalamatas make a good tapenade.

SERVES 8–10
- 250 g (9 oz) black olives, stoned
- 4 tinned anchovy fillets
- 5 tablespoons capers, rinsed
- 2 garlic cloves, chopped
- 2 tablespoons lemon juice
- 1 level teaspoon fresh thyme leaves
- 85 g (3 oz) tinned tuna fish (optional)
- ½ teaspoon freshly ground black pepper
- 75–100 ml (3–4 fl oz) extra virgin olive oil

To make the tapenade, put all the ingredients except the oil in the processor and process in brief bursts to give a slightly knobbly purée. Scrape out into a bowl and beat in the oil. If not using immediately, cover with cling film and store in the fridge, where it will keep for a week or more.

Tapenade and Anchoïade

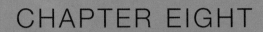

MEAT,
POULTRY
& GAME

FEGATELLI
LIVER AND FENNEL BUNDLES

In the centre of a small, pretty, hilltop village, south of Siena, there is the kind of country restaurant that I, for one, fantasize about. For a start, you have to know where to look for it, since there is absolutely no indication that there is a restaurant at all above the dark grocery. Its one room, with the big, raised hearth in one corner for grilling the home-made sausages and other meats, is warm and relaxed, but on the small side, for, usually, the proprietress is only catering for the locals, lucky souls that they are. We were taken there by a regular, a keen fan of the establishment, as indeed are any who eat there. The Tuscan country food that arrives in such abundance is just unbeatable, made with the best-quality ingredients, grown, raised or made in or near the village. Our host tells us that he always orders the *fegatelli*, typical Tuscan parcels of liver scented with fennel, and, when they arrive, we can understand why. I have never tasted pig's liver so utterly divine. I dare say it has a lot to do with the way the pigs are reared, but the cooking method, too, transforms a humble, and often rather unpleasant, meat, almost beyond recognition.

As far as I could tell the *padrona* does nothing to her liver to tame it but, when I tried the recipe at home, with liver of a lesser pedigree, I found that soaking it in milk works wonders to soften the flavour. You'll have to order the caul fat in advance from your butcher. It's worth buying more than you will need as it is very cheap and freezes well. Not only does it hold the seasonings on the pork but it also bastes the meat as it cooks, keeping it tender and juicy.

SERVES 4-6

500 g (1 lb 2 oz) pig's liver
milk
150 g (5 oz) caul fat
1 tablespoon fennel seeds
extra virgin olive oil, for frying
1 large glass of Vin Santo or sweet white wine
salt and freshly ground black pepper

Cut the pig's liver into pieces about 4 cm (1½ inches) square. Soak in milk for ½–1 hour.

I've usually found that, when I buy caul fat, it is soft and supple and ready to use but, if it is dry and hard, soak in warm water for 5 minutes and then drain thoroughly and open out flat. Cut it, as well as you can, into 10 cm (4 inch) squares.

Drain the pork liver and pat dry. Take a piece of liver, lay it on the centre of a square of caul fat, sprinkle with a good pinch of fennel seeds, salt and pepper. Wrap it up snugly in the caul fat and secure with a cocktail stick pushed right through the parcel. Repeat until all the liver is used up.

Heat enough oil in a frying-pan to fill it to a depth of about 5mm (¼ inch). When the oil is good and hot, fry the fegatelli vigorously, turning frequently, for about 4–5 minutes. When they are done, pour most of the oil out of the pan and quickly add the wine. Bring up to a boil, scraping in any residues from frying, and let it boil down until reduced by about one-third, turning the fegatelli in it so that they are coated in the syrupy juices. Serve immediately.

PAN-FRIED LAMB

WITH CAPER AND RED WINE SAUCE

This is a quick dinner dish of swiftly fried lamb leg steaks, bathed in a sweetish red wine sauce, enlivened by piquant dots of caper. Serve with noodles flecked with parsley, or generous helpings of mash (potato, or mixed celeriac or onion squash and potato spiced with a grating of nutmeg), and braised greens, such as chard or shredded leeks sweated in a little butter or olive oil until tender.

SERVES 4

4 lamb leg steaks
1 garlic clove, halved
2 tablespoons extra virgin olive oil
salt and freshly ground black pepper

FOR THE SAUCE:

150 ml (5 fl oz) good, fruity red wine (a Cabernet
**   Sauvignon holds its colour well)**
1 small fresh rosemary sprig
100 ml (4 fl oz) chicken or lamb stock
2 tablespoons redcurrant jelly
1 tablespoon small capers, or larger ones, chopped
**   (rinsed and soaked if salted)**
salt and freshly ground black pepper

Rub both sides of the lamb steaks with the cut sides of the garlic. Heat the oil in a frying-pan large enough to take all the steaks in a single layer. Lay the lamb in the pan and fry for 2–3 minutes on each side. When the steaks are lightly browned and a tad rarer than you like (they'll continue to cook in their own heat while you make the sauce), lift out on to a warm serving plate, season with salt and pepper and keep warm in a low oven.

Drain excess fat, if necessary, from the pan, then return to the heat. Add the wine and the rosemary. Bring to the boil, scraping in all the brown residues from the meat. Let it boil and reduce to a thin film over the base of the pan. Now add the stock and bring back to the boil. Boil until reduced by half. Stir in the redcurrant jelly, until melted, then stir in the capers. Cook for a further minute or two and then season to taste. Moisten the lamb with a little of the sauce and serve the rest in a jug or sauceboat to pass round separately.

SOUVLAKIA

Never has a kebab tasted so good. We'd boarded the train 36 hours before in rain-sodden Amsterdam but, as we rolled into the first station in Greece, after a sleepless night in an over-crowded compartment, our spirits lifted. The sun was blazing, the platform was noisy and bristling with hawkers of all kinds of sundries, from newspapers and chewing gum to, merciful heavens, sizzling, smoky, herby kebabs. Leaning out of a window, we shouted along with the best of them, gathering those essential provisions and a few moments of warm sun on our heads. As the train rumbled on towards Athens, we settled down to what seemed like a veritable feast.

Souvlakia are the ubiquitous Greek kebab, characteristically but not inevitably made up of rather small cubes of pork or lamb that have been marinated with coriander and *rígani*, the remarkable Greek dried oregano. Make sure that the meat has plenty of time to absorb the flavours of the marinade (24 hours is ideal), and barbecue or grill or griddle them very close to a high heat, so that the exterior cooks to a dark, caramelized brown while the inside, close to the skewer, remains succulent and juicy. Serve them with tzatziki, the characteristic Greek sauce-cum-starter of yoghurt mixed with cucumber, garlic and mint.

SERVES 4–6

1 kg (2¼ lb) boneless leg or shoulder of lamb or pork
1 tablespoon coriander seeds
2 teaspoons *rígani* or dried oregano
150 ml (5 fl oz) extra virgin olive oil
4 tablespoons red wine vinegar
1 onion, grated
2 bay leaves, roughly torn up
salt and freshly ground black pepper

FOR THE TZATZIKI:
½ cucumber, peeled and finely diced
1 tablespoon white or red wine vinegar
150 g (5 oz) thick Greek yoghurt
1 garlic clove, crushed
1 tablespoon finely chopped fresh mint
salt and freshly ground black pepper

Cut the pork or lamb into 2 cm (¾ inch) cubes, trimming off any gristle or other unwanted bits and bobs. Mix all the remaining ingredients and then pour over the meat. Turn so that all the pieces are coated and then cover and leave to marinate for at least 2 hours, but preferably something nearer 24 hours, in a cool place.

To make the tzatziki, spread the cucumber dice out in a colander or sieve and sprinkle over the vinegar and a little salt. Leave to drain for 1 hour. Then pat dry with kitchen paper or a clean tea towel. Mix with the rest of the tzatziki ingredients, taste and adjust the seasoning. Serve either lightly chilled or at room temperature.

Back to the souvlakia. Soak wooden skewers in a bath of cold water for an hour or two and then thread the meat on the skewers. Don't push the cubes right up cheek by jowl one to another, but leave a minuscule gap between each pair, just enough space for the heat to curl round every cube, cooking it evenly. Pre-heat either the barbecue or grill or even an oiled griddle pan (place over a high heat for about 3–5 minutes) and then cook the kebabs close to the heat, or on the griddle pan, turning and brushing occasionally with the leftover marinade, until they are crusty and brown. Serve sizzling hot, with a wedge of lemon and the tzatziki.

ARISTA ALLA FIORENTINA
ROAST PORK, FLORENTINE STYLE

One of the joys of Tuscan food is its proud simplicity, secure in the knowledge that its basic ingredients are of superb quality. Nowhere is this more obvious than in *arista alla Fiorentina* – roast pork, Florentine style. There's nothing particularly unusual about the cooking method – the meat is just roasted gently in the oven – for the recipe relies absolutely on the meat itself, and the pigs around Florence are obviously happy, well fed, free-ranging creatures. I don't think there is really much point in trying it unless you take the trouble to buy high quality, free-range pork: that is more than half the battle won. The only 'tricks' are, first, roasting the meat on the bone, which gives extra flavour and richness, and ample quantities of finely chopped rosemary and garlic, pushed right into the flesh.

Ask the butcher for a loin of free-range pork on the bone (also known as a rack of pork), cut from the thicker end of the loin, so that there is plenty of meat relative to bone. Ask him to trim off most of the fat and skin leaving just a thin layer of fat over the meat. Make sure that he gives you the back fat and skin, which you can wrap around game birds as they roast to keep them moist, or cut into small squares and add to a stew to give a velvety texture to the sauce.

The pork is excellent served with the *Rosemary Roast Potatoes* (yes, more rosemary, but believe me, it doesn't overwhelm) on page 56, or *Fagioli al'Uccelletto* (see page 64). Add some kind of green vegetable – stir-fried spinach perhaps, or green beans – and the meal is easily complete.

SERVES 4–6

1 loin of pork on the bone, weighing 1.25–2 kg (3–4 lb) (see introduction)
3 tablespoons finely chopped fresh rosemary leaves
2 garlic cloves, finely chopped
1 glass white wine (nothing too sharp and acidic)
2 tablespoons extra virgin olive oil
coarse salt and freshly ground pepper

If time is on your side, prepare the joint the day before you want to cook and eat it, so that the scent of the garlic and rosemary has time to make its mark on the meat. Mix the rosemary with the garlic. Make holes in the pork with the blade of a narrow knife, then stuff a little of the rosemary and garlic mixture as deeply as you can into each one. Season the outside of the pork generously with salt and pepper. If you are preparing this a day in advance, cover the joint loosely and transfer to the fridge. Bring back to room temperature before roasting.

Pre-heat the oven to 170°C/325°F/Gas Mark 5. Pour the wine into a roasting tin large enough to take the pork. Place the pork in it, bones downwards so that they form a support for the meat itself. Rub the skin with the extra virgin olive oil. Roast for 2 hours, basting occasionally with its own juices. Add a few good splashes of water to the pan each time you baste, so that the juices do not dry out and burn.

To check that it is cooked, plunge a skewer into the centre (not too near the bone) and pull out – if the juices run clear, then it is ready. Leave the pork to rest in a warm place (you can simply turn the oven off and leave the door ajar) for about 20 minutes.

To carve, use a sharp knife and cut down close to the ribs, sliding the knife underneath the meat, until you reach the long, solid chine bone at their base. Swivel the blade of the knife upwards and guide it over the chine bone and down the other side, to release the meat. Lift the meat off and cut into slices about 2.5 cm (1 inch) thick. Arrange on a plate, cover and keep warm. Quickly put the roasting tin over the heat and bring to the boil, scraping in all the residues on the base and adding a little more water if they taste too strong – you won't end up with a huge amount of pan juices, but just enough to moisten each slice of meat. Pour into a jug, and serve with the meat.

ROAST SPATCHCOCKED CHICKEN
WITH LEMON, GARLIC AND BLACK OLIVE PURÉE

Just totally wonderful as long as you like black olives, which I do. What comes out of the oven is a crisp-skinned, perfumed, tender, salty and lemony bird that anyone in their right mind would want to devour instantly. Serve it with new potatoes, and maybe some *Tomates à la Provençale* (see page 58) or even just a plain tomato and basil salad, if the tomatoes are of good quality.

SERVES 4

1 free-range chicken
1 lemon
175 g (6 oz) black olives, stoned
3 tablespoons roughly chopped fresh parsley
2 garlic cloves, roughly chopped
**75–100 ml (3–4 fl oz) extra virgin olive oil, plus a
    little extra**
coarse salt and freshly ground black pepper

Pre-heat the oven to 190°C/375°F/Gas Mark 5. Now tackle that chicken: turn the bird breast-side down, then, using poultry shears, or a sharp, strong knife, cut along the backbone from neck to tail end. The next move is to snip or cut out the backbone completely, and then remove the wishbone. Turn the chicken skin-side up, then flatten it out firmly with the heel of your hand to form a butterfly shape (well, vaguely, anyway). Oil a roasting tin large enough to take the flattened chicken.

Grate the zest of the lemon finely. Put into a processor with the black olives, parsley and garlic. Process until finely chopped, then gradually trickle in the olive oil, with the blades of the motor still running, until you have a thick cream (you may not need all of it). Scrape down the sides and base and give the whole lot one last blast.

Now the messy bit. With your fingers, separate the skin from the flesh of the bird at the neck end. Wiggle your fingers about inside, pulling away the skin, but leaving it tethered at the sides, to form a pocket over the chicken. Now spoon and smear around two-thirds of the black olive mixture between the flesh and skin, patting it down so that it spreads all over. Squeeze over the juice of half the lemon, and season the skin with salt and pepper, rubbing it in. Finally drizzle over another tablespoon of olive oil.

Roast for 45 minutes, until the chicken is cooked through, basting once or twice with its own juices. Check that it is done by plunging a skewer into the thickest part, between thigh and breast. If the juices run clear then the bird is ready, but if they run pink, it needs more time in the oven.

The chicken will be so tender that it is very easy to tear and cut up into rough portions. Don't try any fancy carving into elegant slices – it just won't work. Keep the helpings rough and chunky and you are on the right track.

DJEJ MAKALI

TAGINE OF CHICKEN, PRESERVED LEMONS AND OLIVES

This is one of the most renowned of Moroccan tagines, those gently spiced stews of meat and vegetables – and often fruit as well – that take their name from the earthenware dish with a conical lid that they are cooked in. One Moroccan cook told me firmly that anything that is cooked in a tagine is called a tagine, not just the stews. You could scramble eggs in it, or cook spaghetti bolognaise and, to a Moroccan, these would then become a tagine.

So, I guess, technically speaking, if you cook this subtle dish of semi-stewed, semi-steamed chicken in a saucepan then it shouldn't be called a tagine at all, just a straight pot-roast. Ah, but what a pot-roast, spiced mildly with ginger, cumin, turmeric and saffron, and with the salty tang of preserved lemons and juicy olives. Unlike a couscous, this is a dish which should end up with just a small amount of sauce, enough to moisten the meat and that's about all, for it is usually served on its own, or perhaps with a selection of salads, but certainly without any starchy accompaniments other than a wedge of bread.

SERVES 4

1 large free-range chicken
1 teaspoon ground turmeric
1 teaspoon ground ginger
1 teaspoon ground cumin
4 garlic cloves, crushed
1 onion, grated
2 chicken livers
1 tablespoon extra virgin olive oil
300 ml (½ pint) water
pinch saffron threads (optional)
1 preserved lemon (see page 132)
110 g (4 oz) pinky red and green olives (assuming you can't get Moroccan ones, try either Gaeta, or Greek Kalamata olives)
salt and freshly ground black pepper

Trim the flaps of excess fat from the chicken at the opening to the stomach cavity, and remove any other lumps of fat you can locate. Truss the bird firmly, by tucking the ends of the legs into the opening and tying them in place with string. Rub the turmeric, ginger and cumin over the chicken, and then smear over half the garlic. Season lightly with salt and pepper, then cover and set aside for up to 12 hours (covered and in the fridge).

Put the remaining garlic, the onion, the chicken livers, the olive oil and water into a casserole or saucepan, or a tagine large enough to take the chicken. Stir and bring to the boil. Now, add the chicken and reduce the heat so that the liquid barely simmers. Cover the pan, leaving just a small gap for steam to escape, and cook for 1½–2 hours, turning the chicken frequently so that the flesh is partially steamed and partially simmered to a melting tenderness.

Meanwhile, soak the saffron, if using, in a tablespoon of hot water. Scrape the pulp out of the lemon and discard. Cut the skin into strips, rinse thoroughly, drain and reserve. Rinse the olives. Bring a pan of water to the boil, add the olives and blanch for 1 minute, to remove excess salt. Drain thoroughly.

When it is done, take the chicken out of the pan, and keep warm. Find the livers, quarter them and reserve them too. Stir the strips of preserved lemon, the olives and the saffron into the remaining sauce in the pan, then simmer for 2–3 minutes. Taste and adjust the seasoning.

Serve the chicken with the sauce spooned over and around it, scattering the bits of liver in amongst the olives and lemon.

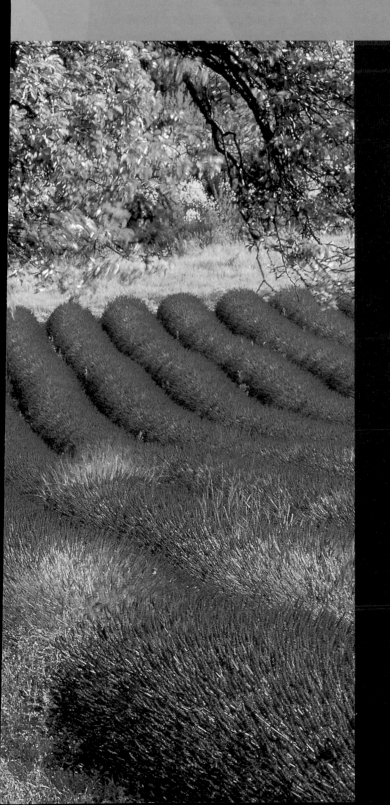

CHAPTER NINE

PUDDINGS
& DRINKS

YOUNG GOATS' CHEESE
WITH HONEY AND TOASTED WALNUTS

I've come across this pudding in one form or another in many of the Mediterranean countries, and I've always enjoyed its purity. Virtually wherever some form of soft cream cheese is made, it is dished up as a quick pudding, topped with nuts and drizzled with honey. Back home, I like it best made with soft, mild goats' cheese or ricotta.

In Greece and Turkey, you might be more likely to come across pots of thick yoghurt, with a delicious thickened crust, topped with dark Hymettus honey (one of the best honeys in the world, made by bees that sup on the flowers of the wild thyme that blankets the slopes of Mount Hymettus) and nuts. If you have a good Greek or Turkish deli nearby, ask for genuine crusted Greek yoghurt. If they don't stock it, the widely sold Greek or Greek-style yoghurt is still pretty damn good served in this way.

SERVES 4

50 g (2 oz) walnut pieces
300 g (11 oz) soft, mild goats' cheese
4 tablespoons milk or single cream
4 tablespoons dark, perfumed honey e.g. Hymettus, chestnut, lavender, etc., plus extra to serve

Pre-heat the oven to 190°C/375°F/Gas Mark 5. Spread the walnuts out on a tray and roast in the oven for about 5–10 minutes, until they have turned a shade or two darker. They can blacken and burn quite suddenly, so check frequently, shaking the nuts every time to ensure even roasting. When they are done, tip into a wire sieve and shake around to dislodge stray bits of papery skin. Leave to cool.

Beat the goats' cheese with enough milk or cream to loosen and soften its texture to a very thick, creamy consistency. Divide between four small bowls. Just before serving, drizzle a tablespoon of honey over each one and then scatter with toasted walnuts. Serve immediately, with extra honey on the table for those with a sweet tooth.

MOROCCAN FIG AND PISTACHIO SALAD
WITH ROSE WATER

This has to be one of the prettiest of fruit salads, especially when made with purple-skinned figs, which set off the green pistachios beautifully. To skin pistachios, cover with boiling water, leave for about 30 seconds, then drain and pop them out of their skins.

SERVES 3–4

8 ripe green or purple figs, quartered
1 tablespoon honey
2 teaspoons rose water
15 g (½ oz) skinned pistachios, roughly chopped
crème fraîche or double cream or whipped cream, to serve (optional)

Arrange the fig quarters on a plate. Warm the honey briefly with the rose water, mixing the two together, then drizzle over the figs. Scatter with the pistachios, and serve at room temperature, with the cream for those who want it.

Young Goats' Cheese with Honey and Toasted Walnuts and Moroccan Fig and Pistachio Salad

TORTA DI PESCHE O PRUGNE
PEACH OR PLUM TORTE

This big, moist Italian fruit cake is a joy in the summer months when peaches and, later, plums are fragrant and plentiful. Some of the fruit is buried in the pale golden crumb, while the rest, scattered generously over the surface, catches and buckles and caramelizes in the heat of the oven. I first caught sight of it in a marvellous delicatessen tucked away behind the heart of Siena. I devoured a slice from a square of waxed paper, walking down a cobbled street, leaving a trail of crumbs behind me for the birds, and never mind the fact that unseasonal, torrential rain was pelting down.

The *torta* is relatively thin, in the Italian style, compared to our own cakes, ready to be eaten in large wedges, on its own, or with mascarpone or whipped cream as the fancy takes you. I find that it improves on keeping, so if you can bear to keep it in an airtight container for 24 hours, you will find it worth the wait.

SERVES 8–10

400 g (14 oz) plain flour
1 level tablespoon baking powder
310 g (11 oz) caster sugar
4 eggs
finely grated zest of 1 lemon
150 g (5 oz) unsalted butter, melted and cooled until tepid
5–6 peaches or nectarines or 8–10 plums, depending on size

Pre-heat the oven to 180°C/350°F/Gas Mark 4. Line the base of a 26 cm (10½ inch) cake tin with non-stick baking parchment, and butter the sides generously. Sift the flour with the baking powder. Reserve 3 tablespoons of the sugar. Whisk the rest with the eggs until the mixture is pale and thick. Fold in the flour and the lemon zest, alternating with the melted butter.

Skin the peaches or nectarines, if using, then halve and remove the stones. If using plums, just halve and remove the stones. Cut the fruit into slices about as thick as a £1 coin. Spoon about half of the cake batter into the prepared tin, and smooth over. Lay about one-third of the fruit higgledy piggledy over the batter, then dollop on the remaining batter and smooth down lightly. Cover with the rest of the fruit, again, higgledy piggledy (oh, well, if you really want straight lines or concentric circles, that's absolutely fine). Sprinkle the reserved sugar over the top. Bake for 55–60 minutes or until a skewer inserted into the centre comes out clean (except maybe for a smear of molten fruit).

Turn out on to a wire rack, and leave to cool. Serve in big wedges; it's lovely on its own and devilishly good as a pudding, with cream or mascarpone.

MSEMME
MOROCCAN LAYERED PANCAKES

We stayed in a hotel in the European quarter of Marrakech, where breakfast turned out to be the culinary highlight. Every morning, in one corner of the vast dining room, a young woman was patiently and expertly folding, stretching and griddling *msemme*. These pancakes, with their thin layers, both crisp and soft in places, were undoubtedly the stars of every guest's breakfast and, when I quizzed our guide later on in the day, he waxed ecstatic about them too. They are easy to make, though a little more time-consuming than either the crumpet-like *B'harrer* (*Moroccan Lacy Pancakes*, opposite), or our own more northerly pancakes. However, children just love dealing with the slippery dough, so rope them in and you'll enjoy the process as much as the eating.

MAKES 20

500 g (1 lb 2 oz) strong bread flour
1 teaspoon salt
1 teaspoon sugar
1 sachet easy-blend yeast
sunflower or vegetable oil, or melted butter
semolina

TO SERVE:

melted butter
runny honey

Begin by making a normal bread dough. Mix the flour with the salt, sugar and yeast. Add enough water to make a soft, very slightly sticky dough. Knead vigorously for 10 minutes, until smooth and silky. Place in an oiled bowl, turning the ball of dough so that it is coated in oil, then cover with a damp tea towel and leave to rise until doubled in bulk.

Push the dough down with your fingertips, then gather up into a ball and knead again briefly to smooth out – about 2 minutes. Pour a small slick of oil or melted butter on to two large plates. Spread the semolina out on a small plate. Pour a little more oil or melted butter into a small bowl. Divide the dough into 20 portions and roll each one into a ball. Place on one of the plates, turning each ball so that it is coated in oil. Place a heavy frying-pan or a griddle over a low–moderate heat.

Oil, or pour melted butter over, the work surface – the trick, I fear, is to be generous with the fat at all stages, so go again for a thin slick of oil. Take the first ball of dough and, using your fingertips first dipped into oil, flatten and stretch it out to form a very thin square (more or less) about 17–20 cm (7–8 inches) across, on the oiled work surface. The dough will be very elastic, shrinking back each time you stretch it, but don't let it get the better of you. Lift it up and dip the centre of the pancake into the semolina, so that the central third of the dough is coated lightly. Lay the dough back down on the plate, semolina-side up, and flip the sides over the semolina, and then the ends, to form a square. Fold the square in thirds again, then put to one side on the second plate to rest for 5 minutes. Continue flattening and oiling and folding more balls of dough, while the first one rests, arranging them side by side, in the order that they are made, so you can always tell which was made first and which last. This way, each folded pancake will get its proper rest.

After its allotted rest time, go back to the first one, and again, using oiled fingers on the oiled surface of the plate, tease and spread it out to form a new square, about 15–20 cm (6–8 inches) across. Lay on the griddle, give it a quick stretch again, and cook gently for some 3–4 minutes on each side, until mottled golden-brown. Serve immediately, allowing the ravenous consumer to drizzle their own pancake with melted butter and honey.

Carry on in much the same way with the rest of the dough, aiming to develop a good working production-line rhythm of stretching and folding, resting and cooking. Before you know it, everyone will be satisfied.

B'HARRER
MOROCCAN LACY PANCAKES

Think of these as an Arab version of the British pikelet or crumpet, or indeed, of the Russian blini (but no caviar or smoked salmon required). These pancakes are served for pudding or breakfast, with honey, butter and orange flower water for those who fancy a touch of flowery fragrance. Napkins are essential to keep clothes clean and wipe away the sticky drizzles that run down chins and fingers.

If you want to serve them for breakfast, make the batter the evening before and leave in the fridge overnight. Allow some 15 minutes or so for the chill to wear off, before letting the mixture hit the frying-pan. If you don't use all the batter at one go, it will keep, again covered with a damp cloth, in the fridge for 24 hours or so.

MAKES AROUND 40
500 g (1 lb 2 oz) strong white bread flour
½ teaspoon salt
1 teaspoon caster sugar
1 sachet easy-blend yeast
750–900 ml (1¾–1½ pints) water
sunflower or vegetable oil

TO SERVE:
melted butter
runny honey
orange flower water

Mix the flour with the salt, sugar and yeast. Make a well in the centre and add 250 ml (9 fl oz) of water. Gradually whisk the water into the flour, adding more as you whisk, to form a smooth, runny batter that has more or less the consistency of double cream. Cover the bowl with a damp cloth and leave to rest at room temperature for about 1 hour.

Shortly before cooking, oil a heavy-based frying-pan or griddle and heat over a medium heat. Stir the pancake mixture, and add more water, if necessary, to thin down to a runny batter. Take small ladlefuls of the batter and pour on to the surface of the pan to form a neat circle, about 10–12 cm (4–5 inches) across. Cook until the upper surface is dry and firm and pitted with holes, rather like a crumpet. If the pancakes are too browned for comfort on the underneath by the time this happens, reduce the heat slightly and add a splash more water to the batter to thin it down a smidgeon, then try again.

Stash the pancakes so that they overlap on a plate, and keep warm (or just hand them straight over to the hungry hordes), while you cook the remaining batter. Put the pancakes on the table with the bowls of melted butter and honey and a bottle of orange flower water, so that people can dress their pancakes as they like. Make sure you get a couple, at least, for yourself.

TORTA DI RISO
BAKED RICE PUDDING CAKE

This is another Sienese dessert, a baked cake of rice pudding flavoured with nuts and candied fruit. If you have any fondness at all for rice pudding – I happen to be very partial to the stuff – then this is for you. Serve it on its own, or with a compote of summer fruits, or in winter maybe some fresh pineapple, sprinkled with a little kirsch or some *Limoncello* (see page 195).

SERVES 8

200 g (7 oz) caster sugar
1 litre (1¾ pints) full-cream milk
1 vanilla pod
300 g (10 oz) long-grain rice
3 eggs
110 g (4 oz) candied peel, finely chopped
60 g (2 oz) pine nuts
60 g (2 oz) pistachios
finely grated zest of 1 lemon
45 g (1½ oz) butter

Set aside 85 g (3 oz) of the sugar. Put the milk, vanilla pod and remaining sugar into a pan and bring to the boil. Add the rice and simmer gently until the milk has virtually all been absorbed by the rice, stirring frequently to prevent catching. Leave to cool until tepid.

Pre-heat the oven to 200°C/400°F/Gas Mark 6. Mix the eggs, candied peel, pine nuts, pistachios, lemon zest and butter into the rice. Line the base of a 24 cm (9½ inch) cake tin with non-stick baking parchment, and grease the sides. Spoon in the mixture and smooth down. Sprinkle the reserved sugar evenly over the top. Bake for about 30 minutes, until just firm. If you want a more richly browned top, place under a pre-heated grill for a few minutes until the sugar on top has caramelized. Let the *torta* cool in the tin, then unmould on to a plate.

BAKED LUCCAN FRUIT SALAD

This is a simple dish to make and, once you've got the gist of it, you don't really need a recipe at all. It can be endlessly adapted to use whatever fruits are available in the shops or your garden. As long as you fill the dish well, add a thick layer of sugar, and a good dash of alcohol once it is cooked, you can make it in greater or lesser quantity to fit the occasion.

SERVES 8

2 oranges
3 apples
3 pears
1 pineapple
2 bananas
250 g (9 oz) brown sugar
75 ml (3 fl oz) brandy or Grand Marnier

Pre-heat the oven to 220°C/425°F/Gas Mark 7. Line a large ovenproof dish with a double layer of foil. Divide the oranges, skin and all, into eighths. Core the apples and pears and cut into eighths. Peel the pineapple, and dice, discarding the woody core. Peel the bananas and cut into chunks about 4 cm (1½ inches) long. Mix all the fruit together well and pile into the dish.

Dredge with brown sugar. Bake for 1 hour, turning the fruit in its juices every 15 minutes. Pour brandy or Grand Marnier over the fruit and leave to cool, basting occasionally with the juices.

Serve at room temperature with mascarpone, mixed with a little cream or milk to soften it.

KOURAMBIETHES

ORANGE FLOWER AND ALMOND SHORTBREADS

These roly-poly, crescent-shaped biscuits from Greece are as melting and crumbly as the very best shortbread, with the added delight of a fine layer of icing sugar coating the exterior, held in place with a waft of orange flower water. It doesn't take much imagination to come up with an excuse for eating them but, if you really do need one, bake them one summer afternoon to serve with a bowl of *Poached Peaches* (see page 182).

My first encounter with these wonderful biscuits was in a small dark bakery in the sun-laden port of a Greek island, when I was fourteen. My father was researching a book on the goddess Aphrodite, and his work took us, that Easter, to Greece and Cyprus; so began my love affair with the Mediterranean. Those early, giddy days of young wide-eyed discovery were punctuated with the taste of scented icing sugar licked from sticky fingers.

MAKES 24

250 g (9 oz) unsalted butter, softened
60 g (2 oz) caster sugar
1 large egg yolk
1 teaspoon ouzo, Pernod or brandy
110 g (4 oz) ground almonds
60 g (2 oz) cornflour
300 g (10 oz) plain flour
orange flower water
icing sugar

Pre-heat the oven to 180°C/350°F/Gas Mark 4. Cream the softened butter with the sugar until very pale. Then beat in the egg yolk and the ouzo, Pernod or brandy, followed by the ground almonds and the cornflour. Gradually work in enough of the flour to give a soft, but not sticky, dough (you may not need quite all of it).

Divide into 24 knobs. Roll each one first into a ball and then, on the worksurface, form into a fat crescent shape. Bake on trays lined with non-stick baking parchment for 25–30 minutes, until a very pale biscuity brown. Cool on wire racks.

Pour a generous measure of orange flower water into a small bowl and spread a thick layer of icing sugar on a plate. One by one, dip the biscuits very quickly into the orange flower water, then roll in the icing sugar, coating each one thoroughly. Leave to dry out on a wire rack. If not eating immediately, stash them away in an airtight container, dusting the bottom generously with icing sugar before placing the first layer of *kourambiethes* in it, then dusting each successive layer with icing sugar.

POACHED PEACHES WITH
ORANGE FLOWER WATER

Sort of a Spanish, Moorish recipe, though particularly nice served with Greek *Kourambiethes* (see page 181), crescent-shaped, melting biscuits fleetingly scented with more orange flower water.

SERVES 6

6 peaches

250 g (9 oz) caster sugar

450 ml (15 fl oz) water

zest of 1 orange, pared in wide strips

zest of 1 lemon, pared in wide strips

juice of 1 lemon

2 tablespoons orange flower water

***Kourambeithes* (see page 181), to serve**

If they are ripe, pull the skin off the peaches, otherwise score the skin of each one around the circumference. Put the sugar into a pan large enough to take all six peaches in a single layer. Add the water and stir over a moderate heat until the sugar has dissolved. Add the orange and lemon zest and bring up to the boil. Lower the peaches into the syrup – there should be enough just to cover them but, if the level falls short, quickly make up another batch and pour in a little more syrup. Bring back to the boil, then reduce the heat very low. Cover the surface with a circle of greaseproof paper to keep the peaches from bobbing up, and to reduce evaporation. Poach for some 15–20 minutes, until the peaches are incredibly tender, with their skins well loosened, if they have not been skinned already.

Pull off the skins, if necessary, lift out the peaches, then arrange the fruit in a pretty serving bowl. Boil the syrup hard until reduced by about half to two-thirds, and good and syrupy. Stir in the lemon juice and orange flower water and pour over the peaches. Leave to cool, turning the peaches occasionally in their syrup.

Serve the poached peaches with *Kourambiethes* and single cream or home-made custard, if you wish.

LEMON PANNA COTTA

Panna cotta, 'cooked cream', is a curious name for a dessert that is barely cooked at all, but who am I to split hairs? The cream is heated to boiling point, after all, so I guess that will do. In reality, these small turrets are nothing more nor less than cream jellies, delicately scented with lemon and Marsala.

Panna cotta, from the north of Italy, is an increasingly popular pudding, and hardly surprising. Served with some mildly sharp fruity sauce or accompaniment, it is the perfect end to a good meal.

With leaf gelatine, now available from larger supermarkets as well as delicatessens, the *panna cotta* can be made in 5 minutes or so and then left for a few hours to set. In winter, serve with *Caramelized Blood Orange and Tangerine Compote* (see page 184) and in summer or autumn with a raspberry coulis: just sieve raspberries, add a few squirts of lemon juice and stir in icing sugar to taste, keeping it on the tart side to contrast with the intensely creamy *panna cotta*.

Half-fill a shallow roasting tin with cold water and immerse the leaves of gelatine in it. Leave until needed.

Heat the creams with the lemon zest and sugar until they begin to boil. Draw off the heat and one by one, take the gelatine leaves out of the cold water, slough off the excess and stir the leaf into the cream. Once they have all dissolved, stir in lemon juice to taste, and the Marsala. Rinse out 8 small ramekins or dariole moulds with cold water, but do not dry. Divide the *panna cotta* mixture between them. Cool, then chill until set.

Just before serving, dip the moulds, one at a time, into hot water for 10–30 seconds (metal moulds will need less time than china ones), run a knife around the edge and invert on to serving plates. Serve with some of the orange compote and its juices and maybe a jaunty sprig of mint for colour.

SERVES 8

3–4 leaves gelatine (enough to set 1 pint)
450 ml (15 fl oz) double cream
150 ml (5 fl oz) single cream
finely grated zest of 1 lemon
85 g (3 oz) vanilla sugar or caster sugar
1–2 tablespoons lemon juice
1 tablespoon Marsala
Caramelized Blood Orange and Tangerine Compote
  (see page 184), to serve
8 fresh mint sprigs, to decorate (optional)

CARAMELIZED BLOOD ORANGE AND TANGERINE COMPOTE

In the winter months, when warmth and summer seem long gone and colds and snuffles are rife, eating citrus fruit of one sort or another is particularly consoling. This compote of blood oranges and tangerines (by which I mean any miniature orange, from satsumas and endless new variations through to clemenvillas) refreshes and comforts in one fell swoop. It can be made 24 hours in advance and will come to no harm at all. Eat it on its own, or for smarter occasions with creamy *Lemon Panna Cotta* (see page 183).

SERVES 8, WITH LEMON PANNA COTTA

7 blood oranges
7 seedless tangerines or satsumas or whatever
  small, well flavoured oranges are available
450 g (1 lb) caster or granulated sugar
225 ml (8 fl oz) cold water
300 ml (10 fl oz) hot water
2 cinnamon sticks

Pare the zest from 5 blood oranges. Cut the zest into fine shreds, then blanch for 2 minutes in boiling water. Drain and reserve.

Peel the blood oranges, cutting right down to the flesh with a sharp knife. Slice each orange, saving the juices that are squeezed out. Peel the tangerines (or whatever), and slice them thinly, too. Place all the oranges in a shallow dish, together with the juice.

Put the sugar into a pan (use one with a metallic or white interior, not black, so that you can see the colour of the sugar clearly as it caramelizes) with the cold water. Stir over a moderate heat until the sugar has completely dissolved. Bring to the boil and stop stirring. Boil hard, swirling the pan occasionally to even out hot spots, but never stirring, until the sugar darkens to a hazelnut-brown caramel. Now, at arm's length, pour in the hot water. Beware – the caramel will spit and hiss and bubble up violently. Swirl the pan then stir to make a clear caramel sauce. Add the shreds of orange zest and the cinnamon sticks and simmer very gently for about 10 minutes in the syrup, until the zest is translucent. Pour the syrup and the shreds over the oranges, then leave to cool. Serve at room temperature or lightly chilled.

HELADO DE LECHE MERENGADA
SPANISH CINNAMON ICE-CREAM

This is a cooling Spanish ice-cream, flavoured with cinnamon and lemon zest. Take great care to use just the yellow zest, pared clean of the white pith that can give the ice-cream a slightly bitter note – not altogether unpleasant but, on the whole, better avoided.

When scoops of *leche merangada* ice-cream are served in glasses, doused with iced black coffee, you have what is known as a *blanco y negro*, a rather sophisticated milk shake.

SERVES 6–8
570 ml (1 pint) full-cream milk
300 ml (½ pint) double cream
3 cinnamon sticks
zest of 1 lemon, cut in long strips
150 g (5 oz) caster sugar
3 egg whites
lemon juice
ground cinnamon, to serve

Put the milk, cream, cinnamon sticks, lemon zest and 85 g (3 oz) of the sugar into a pan and bring slowly to the boil. Turn the heat down as low as possible and leave to infuse for 30 minutes. Then cool and strain.

Whisk the egg whites with a generous squirt of lemon juice until they begin to form soft peaks. Now sprinkle on the remaining sugar and whisk again until stiff. Then beat in the cinnamon milk, a little at a time.

Freeze in an ice-cream maker or pour into a shallow container and whizz into the freezer. When the sides are solid but the centre is still not set, break up the sides and push the crystals into the centre. Leave until just set but not yet solid, then scoop out into a bowl (or the processor) and beat hard to smooth out crystals. Return to the container and rush it back into the freezer. Repeat once more if you have the time and patience, then leave to freeze completely. As you serve, dust each helping lightly with ground cinnamon.

CANTALOUP MELON
ICE-CREAM

There is something unexpected about the thought of a melon ice-cream. Melon sorbet ... yes, that's not so surprising, but ice-cream? Well, why not? It's something I remember from a fantastic *gelateria* (ice-cream shop) in the Umbrian hilltop town of Perugia. It was a concept that seemed unlikely but tempting and, as it turns out, I was quite right to be tempted. When made with the aristocratic orange-fleshed cantaloup or charentais melon (they put poor honeydew and its pale-fleshed cousins quite in the shade) it is a fantastic ice-cream that retains a good deal of the freshness of melon.

Choose a large, ripe melon, one which perfumes the air around it with its magic scent. If that marvellous smell is elusive, the melon is far from ripe and there is no point in transforming it into an ice-cream (or eating it at all, for that matter).

SERVES 8
1 large or 2 small, very ripe cantaloup or charentais melons
300 ml (½ pint) full-cream milk
1 vanilla pod
4 egg yolks
100 g (4 oz) caster sugar
300 ml (10 fl oz) double cream, lightly whipped

Quarter the melon(s) and scoop out the seeds. Scoop out the flesh of the melon(s) over a bowl to catch the juice. Process until smooth.

Bring the milk gently to the boil with the vanilla pod and then draw off the heat. Cover and leave for 5 minutes to infuse. Whisk the egg yolks with the sugar until pale and thick. Re-heat the milk until it is almost, but not quite, boiling. Tip on to the eggs, whisking constantly. Set the bowl over a pan of lazily simmering water and stir until the custard has thickened enough to coat the back of a spoon. Lift the bowl off the saucepan, and stir for a few more minutes; then leave to cool. Strain into the melon purée, add the double cream and mix thoroughly.

Churn in an ice-cream-making machine or pour into a shallow container and freeze as for *Helado di Leche Merengada* (see page 185).

Transfer the ice-cream from the freezer to the fridge about 40 minutes before serving, to soften it.

FIG AND ANISE
ICE-CREAM

What a stunning ice-cream this is. One of the best new puddings I've tasted in a long, long while, the harnessing of fig with Pernod and cream is nigh-on miraculous when the figs are plump, heavy and oozing sticky juices. If you can pluck them ripe to bursting, straight from the tree (and that's quite possible in Britain, in a hot summer, when the figs are grown against a sunny south-facing wall) you will be thrilled by this ice-cream. But don't waver if you only have access to imported supermarket or greengrocer's figs. They can still taste very good in mid summer and, even when they've lost their edge and that intense honey sweetness, they will make an excellent ice-cream.

SERVES 4

500 g (1 lb 2 oz) ripe purple or green figs
1 teaspoon lemon juice
**2 tablespoons Pernod, ouzo, anisette or other anise-
   flavoured alcohol**
150 ml (5 fl oz) milk
3 egg yolks
110 g (4 oz) caster sugar
300 ml (½ pint) double cream, lightly whipped

Peel the figs and then chop roughly. Process in short bursts with the lemon juice and the alcohol to make a knobbly purée. Set aside.

Put the milk into a pan and bring to the boil. Meanwhile, whisk the egg yolks with the caster sugar until light and thick. Pour in the milk, whisking constantly. Place the bowl over a pan of gently simmering water and stir until the custard thickens enough to coat the back of the spoon. Immediately lift the bowl off the pan and stir the custard for a few minutes. Leave to cool.

Mix the figs with the custard and fold in the whipped cream. Freeze in an ice-cream machine, or pour into a shallow container and freeze as for *Helado de Leche Merengada* (see page 185).

Transfer the ice-cream from the freezer to the fridge about 40 minutes before serving, to soften it.

ZUCCOTTO

RICH RASPBERRY OR CHOCOLATE BOMBE

Zuccotto is a very rich, boozy, rather impressive Florentine pudding that begins in much the same way as our summer pudding: a basin lined with slices of sponge cake rather than bread. From then on, it couldn't be more different. The cake is soaked in a mixture of brandy and maraschino, then filled with a rich creamy mixture. It needs to be made at least 12 hours in advance, so that the filling has time to set.

I give two alternative fillings here, both ones that my mother favoured. The pink raspberry filling is excellent for the summer time, whilst the chocolate and ricotta one can be made at any time of the year. Incidentally, the word *zuccotto* means 'skull cap'.

SERVES 8–10

around 750 g (1½ lb) *pan di Spagna*, **sponge cake,**
   Madeira cake or pound cake, sliced
60 ml (2 fl oz) brandy
60 ml (2 fl oz) maraschino, kirsch or Cointreau
sifted icing sugar and/or cocoa powder, to decorate

FOR THE RASPBERRY FILLING:

375 g (13 oz) raspberries
110 g (4 oz) caster sugar
250 ml (9 fl oz) double cream
150 ml (5 fl oz) single cream
45 g (1½ oz) darkest chocolate, finely chopped

FOR THE RICOTTA FILLING:

300 g (10 oz) ricotta cheese
about 60 g (2 oz) icing sugar, plus extra to taste
110 g (4 oz) hazelnuts, toasted and finely chopped
110 g (4 oz) chopped candied citron, orange and
   lemon peel
60 g (2 oz) plain chocolate, finely chopped
300 ml (10 fl oz) whipping cream
110 g (4 oz) icing sugar

If you are making the raspberry filling, begin by mixing the raspberries with the sugar. Leave them for a couple of hours, then drain off the juice. Mix the brandy and maraschino or other liqueur, set aside 2 tablespoons of this mixture and add the remainder to the raspberries.

If making the ricotta filling, just mix the brandy and maraschino or other liqueur, again setting aside 2 tablespoons of this mixture.

Take a pudding basin or hemispherical bowl of about 1.5 litre (2½ pint) capacity. Line with cling film. Cut the slices of *pan di Spagna* or other cake into long, thin triangles and use to line the bowl, overlapping neatly and leaving no holes. Sprinkle generously with some of the alchohol mixture.

To finish the raspberry filling, whisk the double cream with the single cream until it holds its shape (if the weather is hot and thundery, take great care not to overwhisk the mixture). Fold in the raspberries and chocolate. Fill the sponge-lined bowl with the raspberry cream.

To finish the ricotta filling, first, beat the ricotta with the icing sugar until smooth, then mix in the nuts, candied peel and chocolate. Whip the cream until just firm, then fold into the ricotta. Taste and add more icing sugar if you think it needs it. Fill the sponge-lined bowl with the ricotta cream.

Once the bowl is filled, cover with more pieces of *pan di Spagna* or other cake, and sprinkle over the last of the alcohol. Cover with cling film and chill in the fridge for at least 12 hours.

Just before serving, take it out of the fridge, unmould and peel off the cling film. Dust with icing sugar and/or cocoa powder and serve.

AYSH EL-SARAYA
BREAD OF THE SERAGLIO

I'm a sucker for romantic names and the image that the name of this pudding conjured up – a host of beautiful women, lounging in the seraglio or harem, picking delicately at this delectable, rich dish scented with both rose water and orange flower water – was too much to resist. I came across it in Anissa Helou's excellent book *Lebanese Cooking* (Grub Street). It's amazing what can be done with a loaf of stale bread.

In the original recipe, Anissa stipulates a round loaf, with a diameter of 20 cm (8 inches), so that one single slice can cover the base of a bowl. When I came to make it, I just couldn't lay my hands on anything like that, so I used an ordinary, good-quality white loaf (not sliced white flannel, which just turns slimy), which seemed, to me, to work extremely well.

SERVES 6

1 loaf day-old white bread, weighing around 400 g (14 oz)
250 g (9 oz) caster sugar
75 ml (3 fl oz) water
1 teaspoon lemon juice
100 ml (3 fl oz) boiling water
1 tablespoon rose water
1 tablespoon orange flower water
350 g (12 oz) clotted cream
15 g (½ oz) pistachio nuts, finely chopped

Cut the crusts off the bread. Tear the crumb into pieces and place in a bowll.

Put the sugar, water and lemon juice into a wide saucepan and stir over a moderate heat until the sugar has completely dissolved. Brush down any crystals that cling to the sides of the pan with a brush dipped in cold water. Once there are no more visible crystals, bring the syrup up to the boil and stop stirring it. Let it boil hard, swirling and tilting the pan occasionally, so that the syrup cooks evenly, until it has caramelized to a hazelnut brown. Now add the boiling water, a little at a time, at arm's length. At first it will spit and splutter furiously at you. Now stir the syrup until the caramel has all dissolved into the water, bring back to the boil and pour over the torn-up bread. Mix and return the bread and syrup to the pan. Cook over a medium heat for a few minutes, mashing the bread with the back of the spoon, until it has soaked up all the syrup. Stir in the rose water and orange flower water.

Spread the bread out in a 20 cm (8 inch) flat-bottomed serving dish, and leave to cool. When it is cold, beat the clotted cream to soften it and then spread thickly over the bread. Scatter with the pistachio nuts and serve at room temperature or lightly chilled.

RICOTTA, CHOCOLATE AND RUM CREAM

This is a quick and easy pudding to whip up in a few minutes, and one that goes down well with a crisp biscuit or two and perhaps some fresh fruit – strawberries or raspberries, for instance. I've also used the cream to stuff figs, which provide a pleasing fresh, juicy contrast to the creamy filling – either quarter the figs, open them up like a flower and put a large dollop of the cream in the centre, or halve them, spoon out a little of the flesh and mix with the ricotta and then sandwich the two halves back together generously with the ricotta.

SERVES 4–6

60 g (2 oz) raisins or sultanas
4 tablespoons rum
500 g (1 lb 2 oz) ricotta cheese
30–60 g (1–2 oz) icing sugar, sifted
60 g (2 oz) plain dark chocolate, chopped
30 g (1 oz) best-quality candied peel, chopped fairly small
cocoa powder
30 g (1 oz) flaked almonds, toasted

Soak the raisins or sultanas in the rum for an hour or two. Beat the ricotta to soften it and then add the soaked raisins and rum, the icing sugar, chocolate and candied peel. Mix together well. Divide between small bowls. Shortly before serving, dust very lightly with cocoa and sprinkle with almonds.

TARTE AU CITRON
LEMON TART

The sharp-sweet rich texture of a lemon tart just oozes the blessings of the Mediterranean sunshine – no wonder it has become such a very popular dessert in restaurants in this country, as well as featuring in one form or another in Provence (often finished with a cloud of meringue, very similar to a lemon meringue pie) and Italy and, quite probably, elsewhere. This version, thickened not only with eggs but also with ground almonds, is enriched with crème fraîche, which anchors it in France; though, if you fancied, you could substitute mascarpone, to move it down into Italy.

It is quite tart, which is how I and my family all like it but, if you have a distinctly sweet tooth, you could add some 30–60 g (1–2 oz) more caster sugar to the filling, or serve it with lightly sweetened whipped cream.

SERVES 8–12

FOR THE SWEET SHORTCRUST PASTRY:
225 g (8 oz) plain flour
85 g (3 oz) icing sugar
pinch salt
110 g (4 oz) chilled unsalted butter, diced
2 egg yolks
1 tablespoon icy-cold water

FOR THE FILLING:
5 eggs
2 egg yolks
225 g (8 oz) caster sugar
60 g (2 oz) ground almonds
juice of 5 lemons
175 g (6 oz) crème fraîche
finely grated zest of 3 lemons
60 g (2 oz) unsalted butter, melted

TO GLAZE (OPTIONAL):
45 g (1½ oz) icing sugar

To make the pastry, you can throw everything into the processor together and process until a crumbly dough is formed. Then tip it out, gather together and knead briefly until all the stray bits of flour are incorporated. Or you can do it the traditional way, as follows. Sift the flour with the icing sugar and salt. Make a well in the centre and add the butter, egg yolks and water. Using the tips of your fingers, work the ingredients together until you have a soft dough. Gather it up into a ball and, if necessary, knead very briefly to even it out. Wrap in cling film and chill for half an hour.

Find a 26–27 cm (10½–11 inch) tart tin. Since this pastry is fairly rich, and liable to tear and stick something rotten, I prefer to roll it out between two large sheets of greaseproof paper. It's slightly harder work but less infuriating. Every now and then, turn the pastry over and lift off what is now the top sheet. Smooth it out, lay it back on the pastry and continue rolling. This way, the paper won't get stuck in minor folds of the pastry. Once you have rolled it out to a circle about 3–5 cm (1¾–2 inches) larger than the tin, peel off the upper sheet of greaseproof paper and then roll the pastry, with its undersheet of greaseproof, loosely around the rolling pin. Lift and lay it over the tin, pastry down, paper up. Push the paper and pastry loosely into place and then carefully peel off the greaseproof. Now ease the pastry into the corners but don't bother trimming off the overhang. Just leave it be. Don't worry about any small tears or splits – just patch them up with a small strip taken from the overhang, and no one will be any the wiser. Prick the bottom all over with the tines of a fork and then chill in the fridge for 30 minutes.

Pre-heat the oven to 190°C/375°F/Gas Mark 5. Line the pastry case with greaseproof paper or foil and weight it down with baking beans. Bake blind for 10 minutes. Then remove the paper or foil and beans. With a sharp knife, trim off the overhang, to leave a neat edge flush with the edge of the tart tin. Return the pastry case to the oven for a further 5 minutes or so, to dry out. Let it cool slightly.

Put a baking sheet in the oven and then reduce the heat to 150°C/300°F/Gas Mark 2.

To make the filling, begin by beating the eggs and yolks with the sugar until the sugar has dissolved. Whisk in the ground almonds. In a separate bowl, gradually whisk the lemon juice into the crème fraîche. Whisk this into the egg mixture and then mix in the lemon zest and the melted butter.

Now, open the oven and half slide out the baking tray on its shelf. Place the lined tart tin on the baking tray and ladle the lemon filling into it. If the shelf is at a slight tilt, support it so that it is level, in order to fill the case properly. You should be able to get nearly all, if not all, the filling into it. Very, very carefully slide the shelf with its cargo of tart tin and filling back into the oven, trying very hard not to spill any of it (not the end of the world if you do, just not ideal). Bake for about 30–40 minutes, until the filling is just about set but still with a slight wobble in the centre.

If you wish to glaze it, put the grill on to heat up some 5–10 minutes before the tart is done. As soon as the tart is cooked, dredge with icing sugar and place under the grill, turning it frequently, until the sugar has melted and browned (some 2–3 minutes should suffice). Take out and leave to cool.

If you have no desire to glaze it, take the tart out, leave to cool and then dust with icing sugar just before serving.

CROSTATA DI ALBICOCCHE
APRICOT TART

'Have apricots; will make tart' seems to be the approved litany right around the northern shores of the Mediterranean. No wonder, for something magical happens when apricots, pastry and sugar are brought together. The simplest of apricot tarts, the kind that you can buy in summer from any decent pâtisserie throughout France, is made with a blind-baked sweet shortcrust pastry case, packed full of halved ripe apricots, dredged with sugar and baked until the edges catch in the heat of the oven. In this one, a little more Italian in style, the apricots are cossetted in a mascarpone custard, flavoured lightly with their own juice. Served warm from the oven, it is sheer bliss.

SERVES 6–8

FOR THE SWEET ALMOND PASTRY:
175 g (6 oz) plain flour
85 g (3 oz) icing sugar
pinch salt
60 g (2 oz) ground almonds
150 g (5 oz) chilled unsalted butter, diced
2 egg yolks
1–2 tablespoons icy-cold water

FOR THE FILLING:
6 tablespoons caster sugar
700 g (1 lb 9 oz) fresh apricots, halved and stoned
110 g (4 oz) mascarpone cheese
1 large egg
15 g (½ oz) plain flour
1 teaspoon vanilla extract
pinch salt
icing sugar, to decorate

To make the pastry, you can throw everything into the processor together and process until a crumbly dough is formed. Then tip it out, gather together and knead briefly until all the stray bits of flour are incorporated. Or you can do it the traditional way, as follows. Sift the flour with the icing sugar and salt and then mix with the ground almonds. Make a well in the centre and add the butter, egg yolks and water. Using the tips of your fingers work the ingredients together, until you have a soft dough.

Gather it up into a ball, and if necessary, knead very briefly to even it out. Wrap in cling film and chill for half an hour.

Meanwhile, sprinkle 30 g (1 oz) of the sugar over the cut sides of the apricots. Turn each one upside-down, on a wire rack over a baking tray to catch the drips, rubbing the sugar in gently as you do. Leave for an hour, allowing their syrup to dribble out. The riper they are the more they will produce, but don't expect torrents!

Bring the pastry back to room temperature. If you want a perfect-looking finish, roll it out between two sheets of greaseproof paper or cling film (see *Tarte au Citron*, page 192) but, if you are happy with a more casual appearance, just press the pastry into a deep 23 cm (9 inch) tart tin with a removable base, pushing it gently right up the sides as evenly as you can. Chill the pastry in the fridge for 30 minutes.

Pre-heat the oven to 190°C/375°F/Gas Mark 5. Line the pastry case with foil or greaseproof paper and weight it down with baking beans. Bake for 10 minutes. Remove the paper and beans and return the tart case to the oven for a further 5 minutes or so, to dry out. Leave to cool. Reduce the oven heat to 180°C/350°F/Gas Mark 4.

To make the filling, whisk the mascarpone with the remaining sugar and all the other filling ingredients. Scrape in the syrup and sugar from the apricots and mix well. Arrange the apricot halves in the pastry case, cut-sides up, packing them in snugly. Pour over the mascarpone cream. Bake for about 45–60 minutes, until the filling has just set.

Eat hot or warm, lightly dusted with icing sugar.

LIMONCELLO

Limoncello was one of southern Italy's best-kept secrets and it is only in the past few years that I have heard it being talked about further afield. It is a simple but marvellous lemon liqueur, made with the zest of lemons, sugar and pure alcohol – which is sold widely both in Italy and in France, precisely for making liqueurs like this and for preserving fruit. Unless you bring the alcohol back from a holiday abroad, you will have to make do with vodka if you want to concoct your own *limoncello*. Since it has a neutral flavour, vodka does very nicely indeed.

It will take at least 5 weeks before your *limoncello* is ready to drink but it is definitely worth the wait. Sipping small glasses of icy *limoncello* on a hot day is an unbeatable way to end a meal, as long as there is little else to do afterwards. It is also rather good drizzled over ice-cream to turn it into a grown-ups-only sort of a pudding. Naturally, anyone with any grain of feeling for the good life would undoubtedly be delighted with a small bottle of home-made *limoncello* as a present.

MAKES 1.25 LITRES (JUST OVER 2 PINTS)
5 unwaxed large lemons
750 ml (1¼ pints) vodka or pure alcohol
200 g (7 oz) granulated or caster sugar
450 ml (15 fl oz) water

Soak the lemons in cold water for 1 hour; then drain and dry. Pare the zest from all five lemons with a vegetable peeler and place in a clean bottle or preserving jar, with a capacity of just over 1.25 litres (2 pints). Pour in the vodka, seal tightly and leave in a cool, dark place for 1 month.

Not quite there yet ... but not far off. After the month of steeping, make a clear syrup with the sugar and water, stirring them together over a moderate heat until the sugar has completely dissolved. Leave to cool completely.

Now pour it into the lemon vodka and shake or stir well to mix. Strain the mixture through a sieve lined with butter muslin or a coffee filter and then pour into clean bottles and seal tightly. Return them to their cosy, dark, cool nook and leave for one more week (or longer, if you can bear it).

Before serving, chill the *limoncello* thoroughly. You can even keep a bottle in the freezer, to make it really icy.

HORCHATA DE CHUFAS
TIGER NUT MILK

Horchata de chufas is a drink made from tiger nuts, which are actually not nuts at all, but little tubers that grow underground. Throughout Spain, in the hot summer months, iced *horchata* is sold in bars and even from dedicated *horchateria*, stands that specialize in the drink. *Horchata* tastes creamy and rich, but is also enormously refreshing. I prefer it not too sweet, though it does require some sugar in it. Tiger nuts, whilst not an everyday commodity, can often be tracked down in health food shops.

MAKES 900 ML (1½ PINTS)
225 g (8 oz) tiger nuts
75 g (3 oz) sugar
finely grated zest of ½ lemon

Wash the nuts well in several changes of water. Soak in water for at least 3 hours, or overnight.

Drain the nuts and liquidize or process them with enough water to give a fine paste. Mix with the sugar, lemon zest and 1 litre (1¾ pints) of water. Leave to stand for 4 hours.

Strain through a muslin-lined sieve, taste and add more sugar, if necessary. Chill until ice cold, then pour into tall glasses and serve.

HOT MOROCCAN 'GINSENG'

In amongst the bustle and business of the huge Djemma el Fna, Marrakech's main square – which comes alive at night with row upon row of food stalls, flanked by snake charmers, scribes, acrobats, storytellers and others trying to earn a crust – there are a couple of stands selling small tots of what was described to me, amidst gales of ribald laughter, as 'Moroccan ginseng'. I doubt that real ginseng had had much to do with the steaming-hot, sweet, spicy drink that I tasted, but it did perk me up no end, even if the implied activities were never realized.

Now I make it occasionally back at home, not just to revive and rev up but because it is a real dream of a warmer on a chilly evening.

SERVES 2
30 g (1 oz) caster or granulated sugar
1 mace blade
1 cinnamon stick
4 cloves
4 cardamom pods
2.5 cm (1 inch) piece of fresh root ginger, sliced
¼ teaspoon freshly grated nutmeg
6 allspice berries
300 ml (10 fl oz) water
1 teaspoon lemon juice

Put all the ingredients, except the lemon juice, into a pan. Bring to the boil, stirring until the sugar has dissolved. Simmer for 5–8 minutes, stir in the lemon juice, then pour through a tea strainer into two small glasses. A few sips and you'll be skipping through the rest of the evening.

OUR KIND OF MINT TEA

TINTO VERANO
RED WINE AND LEMONADE SPRITZER

I'm really none-too-fond of sweet hot drinks. I can't bear sugar in my tea or coffee and neither, it turns out, could the colleagues I was travelling with, last time I went to Morocco. Now this is a bit of an encumbrance because, everywhere you go in Morocco, you are likely to be offered Moroccan mint tea to drink, and Moroccan mint tea is invariably very sweet. The sweetness ameliorates the underlying bitterness of the green tea they use as a base for the mint so, even when we did manage to persuade them to leave out the sugar, it didn't really help matters too much.

Soon, though, we discovered the happy compromise that kept our thirst slaked, our bodies refreshed and our hosts happy. Plain, fresh mint with nothing else added. To my mind, this makes a brilliantly restorative, digestive drink, a real pick-me-up under warm skies. All you do is stuff several handfuls of fresh mint sprigs into a teapot and then drown them in boiling water. After a few minutes, the plain green brew that emerges is just about perfect. No need for lemon and, if you must add some kind of sweetness, a drizzle of honey is the best way to go about it.

In Spain, they drink an incredibly refreshing summer drink called *tinto verano*, 'summer red'. It is the perfect tonic after a hard morning's shopping in the markets or sightseeing and strolling around town or countryside. It is, I suppose, a red-wine spritzer, and a most effective way of zapping up what might not be the best-quality wine, whilst quenching a raging thirst. Just put a few ice-cubes into a tall glass, fill about a third full with dry red wine and then top it up with any not-too-sweet fizzy lemonade. Find a pew in the shade, sit back and contemplate the world going by.

Our Kind of Mint Tea

INDEX

ACKNOWLEDGEMENTS

Sometimes writing a book can be a bit of a lonely experience, but not this one. It is a subject that meets with instant enthusiasm, and many, many people have thrown themselves into the project with great gusto, not least Mary Clyne. We hatched up the idea for the programme and book over a couple of lengthy, giggly and serious phone calls a little less than a year ago. A shared passion for the food of the Mediterranean spurred us on, and I would like to say a big thank you to her, for the many hours of her enormously enjoyable company and for her friendship and support. Of course, once hatched, the plot needed more encouragement and that came from many quarters. My thanks to Jane Root for commissioning the series, and to my lovely editor, Nicky Copeland, for commissioning the book.

At BBC Books I would also like to commend and thank Lara and Sarah, who have taken on the day-to-day organization of turning a manuscript into a real book, and Deborah Savage who has painstakingly read through the manuscript, ironing out the many glitches. Georgia Glynn-Smith and Maxine Clarke have made the photographs look positively, gorgeously edible. My one disappointment is that they are not. Then back at BBC Pebble Mill I would also like to shout a scrumbunctious large merci, grazie, graçias, etc. to Nicola, Oli, Steve, Liz and co. for being fun, clever, patient, incredibly helpful and fantastic to work with and to carouse with in various watering holes across the Med and back in Old Blighty.

Absolutely crucial and marvellous founts of knowledge have been our guides and helpers in Seville, Cadiz, Siena, Morocco (who could possibly forget Fouad Kabbaj?) and the other places we have visited. The chefs and patrons of the many restaurants and bars we have eaten in over the past year have given me a considerable supply of new ideas and, of course, excellent and varied food, and many small producers have given us their time and expertise. Thanks to them all, and to all those cooks and producers all around the Mediterranean who make life so much better for all of those who live there, and for all of us who travel there.

At home, I have had long suffering and cheerful support from Jennine Bierton and Michele King, both well used now to my quirks and well versed in avoiding the stacks of books covering the floors. Wendy Malpass, Vanessa Jones, Annabel Hartog and Claire Parry-Billings have all helped to shop and to test recipes, and their comments have been invaluable. Finally, a big thank you to William, Florence and Sidney, who tries everything and loves pasta above all else.

PICTURE CREDITS

BBC Worldwide would like to thank the following for providing photographs and for permission to reproduce copyright material. While every effort has been made to trace and acknowledge all copyright holders, we would like to apologise should there be any errors or omissions.

All photographs copyright of BBC Worldwide by Georgia Glynn-Smith, except those from Arcaid, pages 140–1 (Joe Cornish); Axiom Photographic Agency Ltd, pages 8, 9 and 52–3 (Chris Caldicott), and page 16 (D. Shaw); Michael Busselle, pages 13 and 124–5; The J. Allan Cash Photolibrary, pages 108–9; Robert Harding Picture Library Ltd, pages 40–1 (Nik Wheeler), 72–3 and 88–9; Images Colour Library, pages 20–1; and Gettyone Stone, pages 168–9.